T0149026

# WITTGENSTEIN STUDIES

THOEMMES

Printed in Great Britain
by Antony Rowe Ltd

WITTGENSTEIN STUDIES

# Wittgenstein's
# Logical Atomism

## JAMES GRIFFIN

THOEMMES PRESS

This edition published by Thoemmes Press, 1997

**Thoemmes Press**
11 Great George Street
Bristol BS1 5RR, England

*US office: Distribution and Marketing*
22883 Quicksilver Drive
Dulles, Virginia 20166, USA

ISBN 1 85506 536 3

This is a reprint of the 1964 edition

Publisher's Note

The publisher has gone to great lengths to ensure the
quality of this reprint but points out that some
imperfections in the original book may be apparent.

# PREFACE

IN this book I consider only some parts of the *Tractatus*, though they are the parts which seem to me of greatest philosophical interest. I explain which they are in Chapter I.2.

I am indebted to Mr. B. F. McGuinness and Mr. D. F. Pears for various sorts of help, but perhaps especially for the example of their own high standards in work of this kind; I should add that I do not know to what extent either accepts the interpretations I advance here. I am also indebted to Miss G. E. M. Anscombe, Professor A. J. Ayer, and Professor G. Ryle for many valuable comments on earlier drafts.

Since there is a bibliography, I have kept footnote references as brief as possible.

J. P. G.

*Christ Church*
*Oxford*

# CONTENTS

# LIST OF ABBREVIATIONS

| | |
|---|---|
| *NL* | *Notes on Logic* |
| *NM* | *Notes Dictated to G. E. Moore in Norway* |
| *Nbk.* | *Notebooks 1914–1916* |
| *LF* | 'Some Remarks on Logical Form' |
| *Bl. Bk.* | *The Blue Book* |
| *PI* | *Philosophical Investigations* |

# I

# INTRODUCTION

## 1. Some History

EARLY in 1912 Wittgenstein went to Cambridge to study logic with Russell. One of the first problems to interest him was: what is the special nature of the propositions of logic? Obviously they differ from empirical propositions, but precisely how do they differ? At first, he had only a couple of suggestions. He wrote Russell:[1]

Logic is still in the melting pot but one thing gets more and more obvious to me: The propositions of Logic contain *only apparent* variables and whatever may turn out to be the proper explanation of apparent variables, its consequences *must* be that there are *no logical* constants.

'$[\phi x. (\phi x \supset \psi x)] \supset (\psi x)$', for example, is a logical proposition,[2] and Wittgenstein thinks that at least these two things must be true of it. First, the $x$'s must be bound, and, second, there can be no such thing as '$\supset$'. It is clear enough what the first remark means. The second, I think, is an early appearance of a point Wittgenstein was to make again and again and which in the end he considered one of his fundamental discoveries: logical constants do not stand for anything in the world.[3] When I say '$\phi a \supset \psi a$', there may be something in the world answering to the '$a$', perhaps even something answering to the '$\phi$' and the '$\psi$', but there definitely is nothing answering to the '$\supset$'. These were good first observations to have made, particularly the second one; and just how promising that was, Wittgenstein soon began to see. A few weeks later he wrote Russell:[4]

[1] Letter 1: Cambridge, 22.6.12; I assign the letters numbers in the order of their appearance in App. III to *Nbk.*; where a date is conjectured, as sometimes is possible from the personal content of the letters, I append '(?)'. The point I shall make with these letters does not require the use of ones with conjectured dates; it could be made, though less neatly, with the remaining. I thank Wittgenstein's literary executors for access to the full version of the letters.

[2] Cf. *NM* p. 107, lines 29–31 (hereafter in the form *NM* 107.29–31).

[3] See *NL* Sect. III, lines 40–52 (hereafter in the form *NL* III 40–52).

[4] Letter 3: Hochreit, Post Hohenberg, Nieder-Österreich, early Aug. (?), 1912.

What troubles me most at present, is not the apparent-variable-business, but rather the meaning of '∨', '⊃', &c. This latter problem is—I think—still more fundamental and, if possible, still less recognized as a problem.

The problem to concentrate on, he now thought, is the meaning of the logical constants. This is not an easy problem to settle in isolation. How can one tell, for example, what the '⊃' in '$\phi a \supset \psi a$' stands for, without knowing what the rest of the formula stands for? '$\phi a \supset \psi a$' is, after all, molecular, and perhaps if one knew how the '$\phi$', the '$\psi$', and the '$a$' had meaning, and how the atomic propositions, '$\phi a$' and '$\psi a$', individually said what they did about the world, then it would be easier to tell what role '⊃' played in the molecular proposition. Something like this, at least, must have crossed Wittgenstein's mind, for a week or so later he was writing to Russell:[1]

I believe that our problems can be traced down to the *atomic* propositions. This you will see if you try to explain precisely in what way the Copula in such a proposition has meaning.

I cannot explain it and I think that as soon as an exact answer to this question is given the problem of '∨' and of the apparent variable will be brought *very* near to their solution if not solved. I now think about 'Socrates is human' (Good old Socrates!).

By copula Wittgenstein means the whole $\phi$-part in '$\phi a$'. He assumes, I think, that it is easy to say how the '$a$' has meaning; it simply stands for an individual. But how does the '$\phi$' have meaning? A few months later he wrote:[2]

I have changed my views on 'atomic' complexes: I now think that qualities, relations (like love) &c. are all copulae! That means I for instance analyse a subject-predicate proposition, say, 'Socrates is human' into 'Socrates' and 'something is human', (which I think is not complex). The reason for this is a very fundamental one: I think that there cannot be different types of things! In other words whatever can be symbolized by a simple proper name must belong to one type.

What he means here should be clearer later on. As far as history goes, though, a number of things are clear already. Wittgenstein was now well into atomic propositions. Here he is into the Theory of Types, and the next few letters show that types remained

[1] Letter 5: late Aug. (?), 1912.      [2] Letter 7: IV Alleegasse, 16.1.13.

probably his chief—at any rate a big—problem for several months. In other words, Wittgenstein's problems about logical propositions had in these early days given way to problems about atomic propositions, and his interests had moved from strictly logical inquiries into the theory of meaning generally.

And here, in the main, his interest rested. He came, understandably, to regard the theory of meaning not simply as the way to answer his earlier, logical questions but as the more important subject altogether. Everything he wrote subsequently shows this. Consider, for instance, the *Notes on Logic*, which he wrote early in 1913. The first section explains the sense of propositions (the example is '*aRb*'), and here Wittgenstein introduces the *ab* notation (which becomes the *TF* notation in the *Tractatus*). The second section is about atomic propositions: what are their components? How do these components differ? What symbolizes in an atomic proposition? It is not until the third section that molecular propositions are taken up, and then they are explained in terms of the *ab* notation introduced in the first section to explain the sense of atomic propositions; logical propositions do not, in any explicit way, get taken up at all. Or take, say, the *Notebooks 1914–1916*. They mention logical propositions only rarely; instead the important subjects here are: in what sense must there be simples, either simple objects or simple (i.e. atomic) propositions? What must be common between fact and proposition in order for the second to describe the first?

## 2. *My Subject*

Now, my subject in this book is just the set of questions, centring on atomic propositions, which in these early days Wittgenstein came to regard as fundamental. (I leave it open for now whether he still thought this way in the *Tractatus*.) It is a *set* of questions, because one cannot discuss atomic propositions without also discussing atomic facts (in the *Tractatus*, 'Sachverhalte'); nor names without discussing objects ('Gegenstände'); nor names without also discussing how they differ from functions; nor names and functions without discussing types (in the *Tractatus*, the Doctrine of Showing); nor either atomic propositions or facts without discussing how they are related (in the *Tractatus*, the Picture Theory); nor anything *atomic* without discussing how and why we analyse the *non-atomic*.

In discussing these subjects I begin with the pre-*Tractatus* writings (Chapters II–IV). I give them so much attention, because patience with historical matters, however tedious, is necessary with the *Tractatus*. Half the battle is sometimes won just by knowing that here in the *Tractatus* Wittgenstein is arguing against this in Frege or that in Russell, or that such-and-such in the *Tractatus* is Wittgenstein's renovation of Russell's Theory of Types or his expansion of Frege's *Grundgesetze* theory of definition. With the *Tractatus* itself I follow closely the outline of Wittgenstein's argument. The majority of the subjects I discuss come in the 1's, 2's, and 3's, and in the six chapters I give to the *Tractatus* (Chapters V–X) I simply divide the 1's, 2's, and 3's into what seem to me to be their six main parts, which then I take up in order. There are several sections in the 4's, and some in the 5's and 6's I also consider, but I bring them in in connexion with one of the parts of the 1's, 2's, or 3's. In a final chapter (Chapter XI) I summarize the two themes of this book: why the old interpretation of the *Tractatus* is wrong, and what the new interpretation should be.

By the 'old' interpretation I mean Russell's and the Vienna Circle's: that is, the interpretation which makes Wittgenstein's elementary propositions into Russell's atomic propositions or Carnap's protocol sentences, which takes propositions of the 'this red now' variety as elementary, and which considers analysis as analysis into units of experience. The important thing about this interpretation is that it places the *Tractatus* in a certain philosophical tradition; it presumes that Wittgenstein shares the common philosophical belief that only immediate experiences are really reliable, and that everything else we speak of is reliable only to the extent that it is built up out of immediate experiences. It presumes that elementary propositions are important because they are what is especially immune from doubt, and that analysis is important because it is the way to reach what is, as knowledge, most certain.

Parts of this old interpretation are easy to attack. To attack the 'this red now' example all that one need do, as Anscombe shows,[1] is cite 6.3751c: 'It is clear that the logical product of two element-ary propositions can neither be a tautology nor a contradiction. The statement that a point in the visual field has two different colours at the same time is a contradiction.' Hence, 'this red now' is not elementary. This is a start. But all the rest of the interpreta-tion has to go too. The trouble with 'this red now' is nothing minor; reformulation, a bit more analysis, will not make it do. It has been fished out of the wrong philosophical stream, and what must be shown, therefore, is that the whole presumption about the tradition the *Tractatus* belongs to is mistaken.

This is one aim; the other is to provide a new interpretation. In the *Tractatus* Wittgenstein was not so much an epistemologist as a logician with a strong bent towards the sciences. The two predecessors most useful to keep in mind in reading the *Tractatus* are a mathematician and a physicist, Frege and Heinrich Hertz. Frege's influence was the more important. But it was influence on the content of the *Tractatus*, not its form. Frege was not a systematic philosopher, in that sense of the word in which the *Tractatus* is a highly systematic work. The important influence on the form, I think, was Hertz's. In *The Principles of Mechanics* Hertz gives the characteristics which any language for the descrip-tion of the world (from the mechanical point of view) must possess. Wittgenstein models so much of the *Tractatus* on this work that there is point to thinking of the *Tractatus* as *The Principles of All Natural Sciences*. The *Tractatus* too aims at setting up principles for language, but they are the principles governing, not a particular kind of report, but any report about the world; and the reports in the *Tractatus* are *about the world*, not about experience, and not about sense-data. We made a mistake in not paying more attention to Wittgenstein's biography; he came to philosophy from engineering via mathematics, a fact which has left more of a mark on the *Tractatus* than we have yet recognized.

[1] G. E. M. Anscombe: *An Introduction to Wittgenstein's Tractatus*, p. 27.

# II
# ATOMIC PROPOSITIONS

## 1. *Introductory*

THE way to understand elementary propositions in the *Tractatus* is first to master atomic propositions in the pre-*Tractatus* material, which is what I try to do in this chapter. I have picked three of their features which seem to me most important. Before beginning, though, I should make one thing clear: I pick passages from the pre-*Tractatus* material because I think they are helpful in understanding the *Tractatus*. They do not necessarily express *Tractatus* views. Some do; some do not; and for now I am not interested in drawing the distinction.

## 2. *Their Indefinable Parts*

One of Wittgenstein's concerns in *Notes on Logic* is with indefinables. He wants both to establish that some symbols must be indefinable, and then to explain how symbols which are indefinable get their meaning. The first point he argues for as follows:[1]

We must be able to understand propositions we have never heard before. But every proposition is a new symbol. Hence we must have *general* indefinable symbols; these are unavoidable if propositions are not all indefinable.

This is a very condensed step-by-step argument. The first step goes: we do as a matter of fact understand propositions we have never met before; all theories of symbolism must be able to explain this fact. The second step: every proposition is a new symbol. Not every proposition is 'new', of course, in the sense of 'never met before', because particular combinations of words can be met for second, third, &c., times. Wittgenstein must mean, I think, that every proposition is as good as new; we do not remember propositions as wholes; we know the meaning of the elements and the rules for their assembly; and since it is only this knowledge that is used on any occasion in understanding a proposition,

[1] *NL* II 13–16.

propositions are always in effect new symbols. It is not by acquaintance that we know what a proposition means. The third
step: hence, we must have general indefinable symbols. Here,
clearly, some steps are missing. What are *general indefinables*?
Are there also *particular indefinables*? General indefinables, both
this argument and certain other passages suggest,[1] are things like
'$\phi x$' or '$xRy$'. This would seem to make names the particular
indefinables. It is clear enough that Wittgenstein regards names
as indefinable, for he asserts it without argument.[2] No one, he
appears to think, would claim that we understand names because
we can give definitions of them. But what of functions? The
argument seems to move like this. We understand propositions,
not by being acquainted with what they are about, but by understanding their constituents. And how do we understand the constituents? Through definitions? As far as names go, obviously not.
Now comes the third step. And as far as functions go, some have
to be indefinable, for otherwise, to use Wittgenstein's words, all
propositions would be indefinable. This is so, because:[3]

Only the doctrine of general indefinables permits us to understand the
nature of functions. Neglect of this doctrine leads us to an impenetrable
thicket.

Suppose the function were '$x$ is a triangle', and suppose we rejected
the doctrine of general indefinables. Then we must say that we
understand this function because we can define it. We define it as:
'$x$ is a plane figure bounded by three straight sides'. But then we
understand '$x$ is a triangle' only if we understand '$x$ is in a plane',
'$x$ is a figure', '$x$ is bounded', &c., all of which are still functions.
So we have now to define all of these, and so on without end.
This infinite regress, I take it, is the 'impenetrable thicket'.
There must be indefinable functions; otherwise one lands in this
familiar regress. Otherwise, too, all propositions would be indefinable; that is to say, some propositions are understood because
we can define them (i.e. define their constituents), and were there
not some propositions which did not have to be defined (i.e. with
constituents that needed no definition), then no proposition could

[1] See *NL* II 19–22, 23–29; see also Letter 7: IV Alleegasse 16.1.13.
[2] See *NL* II 21.     [3] *NL* II 16–18.

be understood. Propositions cannot go on forever depending upon other ones for their meaning.

This is a fairly familiar argument. What is new in Wittgenstein's remarks comes when he explains how indefinables get their meaning. Again the case of names is taken as obvious, and that of functions contrasted with it. He asks us to consider:[1]

> . . . symbols of the form '$xRy$', to which correspond primarily pairs of objects of which one has the name '$x$', the other the name '$y$'. The $x$'s and $y$'s stand in various relations to each other, and among other relations the relation $R$ holds between some but not between others. I now determine the sense of '$xRy$' by laying down the rule: when the facts behave in regard to '$xRy$' so that the meaning of '$x$' stands in the relation $R$ to the meaning of '$y$', then I say that these facts are 'of like sense' (*gleichsinnig*) with the proposition '$xRy$'; otherwise 'of opposite sense' (*entgegengesetzt*). I correlate the facts to the symbol '$xRy$' by thus dividing them into those of like sense and those of opposite sense. To this correlation corresponds the correlation of name and meaning. Both are psychological.

Names, the particular indefinables, are correlated with their 'meaning', where for 'meaning' we can, I think, read 'Bedeutung'. Thus, for what clarity it adds, Wittgenstein's position here appears to be the same as it is in the *Tractatus*, viz. the meaning of a name is the object with which it is correlated. Now, general indefinables, like '$xRy$', also get their meaning through being correlated with something in the world, but this correlation, it would seem, is more complicated. There are in the world various pairs of objects, which pairs separate naturally into those standing in a particular relation to one another and the remaining pairs which are not, and pairs standing in another particular relation and the remaining pairs which are not, and so forth. That is, I look at the facts, and I see where they naturally divide. Now, I give '$xRy$' a sense by correlating it with a group of pairs which stand in a particular relation and also with the group of the remaining pairs which do not stand in this relation. I make the correlation by laying down the rule that the first group of pairs will be 'of like sense' with '$xRy$' and that the second will be 'of opposite sense'. Thus, names and functions are alike in that each is correlated with something in

[1] *NL* II 31–42.

the world, and that this correlation is what gives them their meaning. But a function is not just another sort of name. A name is correlated with a single object; naming, in effect, is labelling. A function, on the other hand, is correlated with a group of facts. But the function is not the label of the group of facts; it does not *mean* or refer to that group of facts. On the contrary, it is the part of the proposition that makes the assertion; it says that a certain pair of objects is *of like sense* with a number of facts which, as a matter of psychology, I correlate with that function.

### 3. *Their Simple Parts*

But how is the subject of indefinability related to the main topic of this chapter, atomicity? They are related because Wittgenstein maintains, first, that indefinables are simple symbols, and vice versa, and, second, that atomic propositions contain simple symbols alone. Now, to understand why he should maintain both these things, it is best to go back to a certain argument of Frege's.

Frege was disturbed by a practice some mathematicians had of introducing a concept, say that of '$x$ equals $y$', for the positive integers, and then later of reintroducing it for the negative integers and zero, and then later, whenever the number system was again extended, of reintroducing it yet again for the class of numbers just admitted. Frege called this practice 'piecemeal definition', and he argues at length in the *Grundgesetze* that such procedure is improper. He says:[1]

A definition of a concept (of a possible predicate) must be complete; it must unambiguously determine, as regards any object, whether or not it falls under the concept (whether or not the predicate is truly assertible of it). Thus there must not be any object as regards which the definition leaves in doubt whether it falls under the concept. ... We may express this metaphorically as follows: the concept must have a sharp boundary. ... To a concept without sharp boundary there would correspond an area that had not a sharp boundary-line all round, but in places just vaguely faded away into the background. This would not really be an area at all; and likewise a concept that is not sharply defined is wrongly termed a concept.

Frege has, as far as I can find, three different arguments to support

[1] Frege: *Grundgesetze der Arithmetik*, vol. ii, sect. 56 (G & B, p. 159); cf. *PI* para. 71.

this conclusion. (i) Were a definition not complete, he says, then the concept defined could not be recognized as a concept by logic since precise laws would not hold for it.[1] One which will not hold, for example, is the law of excluded middle, which is, according to Frege, just another form of the requirement that concepts be *completely* defined. If the function '$xRy$' were not completely defined, then there would be some pairs of $x$'s and $y$'s for which it had not yet been determined what their standing in the relation $R$ to one another meant; thus, for some values of '$x$' and '$y$' the law '$(xRy) \lor \sim (xRy)$' would not necessarily be true. Then, (ii), just to the extent that concepts are not completely defined, to that extent we will not have definitive propositions.[2] Frege's example is the proposition 'there is only one square root of 9', when 'square root' has been defined for positive integers only. In this case the proposition is true, but only so long as we limit consideration to the positive integers. And because of that limitation the proposition is not definitive. In a short time it may be false, since in a short time we may wish to expand the number system beyond positive integers and so extend the use of the concept 'square root'. Therefore, unless we know that the concept we are dealing with has its range of applicability determined completely, once and for all, then no proposition involving that concept is definitive, either finally true or finally false. And this unstable state of affairs would not be confined to mathematics. Consider the proposition 'there is only one red thing in this room'. If it is undetermined for some sorts of things what it would be for them to be 'red', then the truth or falsity of this proposition can change as the range of the determinateness of the concept changes. Finally, (iii), if we give a concept two or more definitions and so introduce it on two or more separate occasions, then we are 'left in doubt' whether the defini- tions contradict one another or not.[3] If we have one definition of the concept, we have one boundary; that is, we have a single criterion for parcelling objects into the following three groups: (a) those falling under the concept, (b) those not falling under the concept, and, should this be an incompletely defined concept, (c)

---

[1] *Grundgesetze der Arithmetik*, p. 159; see also p. 166.
[2] Ibid., pp. 164–5.        [3] Ibid., pp. 160–3.

those for which it is undetermined whether they fall under the concept or not. Then, if we have another definition of the same concept, we have another boundary, another criterion for parcelling objects into two groups (if this should be a complete definition) or three groups (if it is incomplete). The big question in such a case is: how are these boundaries related? Are they congruent or not? And Frege's answer is: we just do not know, 'we are left in doubt'.[1]

These considerations first make their appearance in Wittgenstein's writings in *Notes on Logic*, in a passage which, with changes, comes over to the *Tractatus* as 5.451:[2]

The indefinables of logic must be independent of each other. If an indefinable is introduced, it must be introduced in all combinations in which it can occur. We cannot, therefore, introduce it first for one combination, then for another; e.g., if the form $xRy$ has been introduced, it must henceforth be understood in propositions of the form $aRb$ just in the same way as in propositions such as $(\exists xy).xRy$ and others. We must not introduce it first for one class of cases, then for the other; for it would remain doubtful if its meaning was the same in both cases. . . . In short, for the introduction of indefinable symbols and combinations of symbols the same holds, *mutatis mutandis*, that Frege has said for the introduction of symbols by definitions.

The difference to which the '*mutatis mutandis*' refers is that, as the last sentence shows, whereas Frege demands completeness in *definition* of *concepts* Wittgenstein demands it in *introduction* of *indefinables*. Indefinables get their meaning, as we saw, by being introduced in a certain way into the symbolism, and, Wittgenstein adds here, they must be *completely* introduced. Now, though he may be in sympathy with all three of Frege's arguments, he uses only the third, which in his case runs like this. We know the meaning of, say, a function through its being correlated with a group of facts which are 'of like sense' with it. But were the function re-introduced and so correlated with another group of facts, we would be left in doubt as to the similarity of meaning until we could assure ourselves that the two groups of facts were themselves, so to speak, 'of like sense' with one another. Thus, an indefinable must be introduced on one occasion, and then for all

---

[1] Ibid., p. 163.    [2] *NL* v 7–19; cf. *Bl. Bk.*, pp. 19, 27.

of its possible combinations. And, thus, to know the sense of an indefinable means that one knows all its combinations: these cannot be separate items of knowledge. The range of applicability of a symbol is not something one need discover about the symbol in addition to understanding its sense; they come together. In other words, this is much the same point as Wittgenstein makes in the *Tractatus* when he says:[1]

If I know an object I also know all its possible occurrences in states of affairs.

These are in themselves important conclusions, but it is their implications for simples and indefinables which for now I want to stress. Propositions, of course, are always complex symbols.[2] But what about the components of propositions? They are simple if they are indefinable; otherwise they are complex. Thus, the test for the simplicity of a symbol is whether or not the symbol is indefinable. What shows this is the passage where Wittgenstein says:[3]

A complex symbol must never be introduced as a single indefinable. Thus, for instance, no proposition is indefinable. For if one of the parts of the complex symbol occurs also in another connection, it must there be reintroduced. And would it then mean the same?

A complex symbol, by definition, is a symbol which can be analysed into parts which themselves are symbols. The '*Rb*' in '*aRb*' would be such a symbol, because both the '*R*' and the '*b*' can appear separately as symbols. Wittgenstein argues that '*Rb*' could not be introduced as a single indefinable. Since its parts can appear separately, they can be reintroduced as indefinables. But for all of the reasons just given, a symbol cannot be introduced twice. Thus, one result of Wittgenstein's adoption of Frege's completeness rule is that no complex symbols can be indefinable. This makes clear a feature of indefinables which Wittgenstein earlier left obscure. All indefinables are simple. And the converse, though Wittgenstein does not explicitly mention it, must also be true. If a simple symbol were definable, then it would also be

---

[1] 2.0123a; see also 2.0121, 2.0122, 2.01231, &c.
[2] *NL* IV 6–9, V 1–5.　　　　[3] *NL* V 38–41.

analysable, *per impossibile*, into the symbols which define it. Simples and indefinables must be one and the same.

## 4. *Their Formal and Material Parts*

The first remark Wittgenstein makes about indefinables is that:[1]

Indefinables are of two sorts: names and forms.

The names are, of course, the '*a*' and '*b*' in '*aRb*' and the '*a*' in '*φa*';[2] the forms are the '*xRy*' in '*aRb*' and '*φx*' in '*φa*'.[3] I want now to ask: why does Wittgenstein divide the atomic proposition into just these components? Why, particularly, does he adopt the curious position that '*xRy*' and '*φx*' are forms of propositions?

These questions connect, in a way that it is best to explain now, with one of the most serious difficulties the *Tractatus* presents an interpreter. There seem to be two equally clear yet inconsistent trends in the *Tractatus*. A state of affairs ('Sachverhalt') is defined as a combination of objects,[4] which would seem to mean that every state of affairs is composed of at least two objects. There is a great deal of talk in the *Tractatus* to confirm this. For instance, the structure of the state of affairs is defined as the way the constituent objects are connected,[5] and how can one have *connexion* unless there are at least two objects? Wittgenstein's chain analogy puts this even more strongly. The objects in a state of affairs fit into one another like the links of a chain,[6] and there must be at least two links to a chain before one gets any *fitting into one another* But this hardly needs labouring, since nearly everyone reads the *Tractatus* this way. There is, however, another series of deductions the *Tractatus* seems to permit. Nothing can correspond to a name but an object; an object is the meaning of a name.[7] There can be nothing corresponding to the object but a name, because objects can only be named.[8] This does leave open the possibility that some objects might not, perhaps cannot, have names, but it closes the possibility that such objects will ever have anything standing for

---

[1] *NL* II 8.     [2] *NL* II 32–33, VI 15–16.
[3] Regarding '*xRy*': *NL* II 28–29, 30–33, 42–43; V 10–13. Regarding '*φx*': *NL* VI 15–16, 38–40.
[4] 2.01.     [5] 2.032.     [6] 2.03.     [7] 3.203.     [8] 3.221.

them in propositions, since objects can only be named. Then we are told at 4.24:

Names are the simple symbols: I indicate them by single letters ('$x$', '$y$', '$z$').
I write elementary propositions as functions of names, so that they have the form '$fx$', '$\phi(x, y)$', &c.

Names are things like '$x$', '$y$', '$z$', and propositions things like '$fx$' and '$\phi(x, y)$'. Thus 4.24 implies that a proposition like '$fx$' has only one name in it, and thus it implies—obviously—that the state of affairs corresponding to it can have only one object in it. The trouble is with subject-predicate sentences. If the state of affairs corresponding to the elementary proposition '$\phi a$' must contain two objects then '$\phi a$' must contain two names, and so '$\phi$' must in some sense be a name. Clearly enough; but just as clearly '$\phi$' is not a name. Right now I do nothing more than raise this problem, for it to be kept in mind in what follows.

What are the components into which an atomic proposition can be analysed? Names and forms, Wittgenstein answers, and I think he means something like this. He distinguishes between the 'components' and the 'constituents' of propositions.[1] Constituents are names; components are names, qualities, or relations. My guess is that Wittgenstein uses the word 'constituent' to suggest the actual ingredients of propositions, and that he thinks of the word 'component' as the vaguer, more general word, meaning it to include not only the ingredients but the way the ingredients are arranged. I think, in other words, that Wittgenstein means it literally when he says that '$\phi x$' and '$xRy$' are forms. '$\phi x$' and '$xRy$' are not among the ingredients from which an atomic proposition is made; they are, on the contrary, part of the way the ingredients, the names, are arranged. Now, this is certainly strange. Properties and relations are on the face of it as much ingredients as names are, and certainly most logicians do not include the $\phi$- or the $R$-part of the propositions in what they mean by *form*. Russell, for instance, uses 'constituent' and 'form' like this:[2]

---

[1] *NL* 1 17–18.
[2] Russell: *Our Knowledge of the External World*, p. 52; see also pp. 60–61.

In every proposition and in every inference there is, besides the particular subject-matter concerned, a certain *form*, a way in which the constituents of the proposition or inference are put together. If I say 'Socrates is mortal', 'Jones is angry', 'the sun is hot', there is something in common in these three cases, something indicated by the word 'is'. What is in common is the *form* of the proposition, not an actual constituent. . . . Take (say) the series of propositions, 'Socrates drank the hemlock', 'Coleridge drank the hemlock', 'Coleridge drank opium', 'Coleridge ate opium'. The form remains unchanged throughout this series, but all the constituents are altered. Thus form is not another constituent, but is the way the constituents are put together.

This clearly enough shows the difference. Russell takes '$\phi x$' and '$xRy$' as *constituents* which, when they appear in a proposition, are given a *form*; Wittgenstein, as I have said, takes them not as ingredients which have a form, but as the form.

This contrast between Wittgenstein and Russell is made the more striking by the fact that Russell seems to have intended this passage as an interpretation of Wittgenstein, in fact, perhaps of just that portion of *Notes on Logic* with which I have contrasted it. In the Preface to *Our Knowledge of the External World*, from which this passage comes, Russell acknowledges an indebtedness to Wittgenstein. Since these lectures were written before the spring of 1914, the largest debt must have been to *Notes on Logic*. Further, and more conclusively, Russell makes the same point again in his 1918 lectures, *The Philosophy of Logical Atomism*,[1] and in these lectures he almost certainly thinks he is interpreting or developing Wittgenstein's ideas.[2] This is not at all an inconsequential disagreement. In taking '$\phi x$' and '$xRy$' as constituents, Russell was also inclined to take them as a kind of name, and this tendency, I think, is the source of the main divergence between his and Wittgenstein's logical atomism. Wittgenstein continued to distinguish sharply between names and functions; Russell continued to assimilate them.

Wittgenstein reached his view largely as a result of deciding that symbols, particularly functions:[3]

. . . are not what they seem to be. In '$aRb$' '$R$' looks like a substantive but it is not one. What symbolizes in '$aRb$' is that $R$ occurs between $a$ and

[1] Russell: *The Philosophy of Logical Atomism*, see esp. p. 196.
[2] Ibid., Preface, p. 177.        [3] *NL* II 52–55.

*b.* Hence '*R*' is *not* the indefinable in '*aRb*'. Similarly in '*φx*' '*φ*' looks like a substantive but is not one . . .

A substantive's role in a sentence is to represent;[1] a substantive is, as it were, the deputy in a proposition for an object in the world. A function is quite different. For example, the '*R*' in '*aRb*' differs from '*a*' and '*b*' in that *it* is not what symbolizes; what symbolizes is that it comes between the '*a*' and the '*b*'. That is, what symbolizes in '*aRb*' are (i) the sign '*a*', (ii) the sign '*b*', and (iii) the *fact* that '*R*' comes between '*a*' and '*b*'. Propositions must themselves be facts, the facts that their constituents have a particular arrangement.[2] Thus, the function-part of a proposition is a fact, while a name is not. Also, it is by making a certain thing the case in a propositional sign that I say that a certain thing is the case in the world.[3] Thus, while names *stand for* objects, arrangements of names *say something* about them; names represent, functions assert.

This begins to explain why Wittgenstein calls '*φx*' and '*xRy*' forms. The trend of his thoughts comes out most clearly in statements like this:[4]

Propositions, which are symbols having reference to facts, are themselves facts (that this inkpot is on this table may express that I sit in this chair).

Language is not essential to propositions. All that is necessary is that there be objects in the proposition (inkpot and table) to stand for the objects in the fact (Wittgenstein and his chair), and that there be arrangement of the objects in the proposition (the one on top of the other) to express that the things in the fact are arranged in a certain way (the one sitting on the other). To objects correspond objects, to arrangements arrangements, and the '*R*' in '*aRb*' is part of the arrangement side of the proposition. It is, in the conventions of our symbolism, one of the devices we use in giving the proposition its arrangement. On different conventions it could be dispensed with. Suppose language were concerned simply with saying how material objects stood spatially to one

---

[1] In *NL* Wittgenstein uses two words: names 'denote' (II 27) or 'designate' (V 24).
[2] See *NL* II 11–13, V 49–54.       [3] See *NL* V 52–54.       [4] *NL* II 11–13.

another. '*aRb*', we could say, means '*a* is to the left of *b*'; '*aSb*' means '*a* is on top of *b*'; and so on. But we could also adopt the convention that the spatial arrangement of the names in the propositional sign is to duplicate the arrangement of the objects in the fact. '*ab*' would mean '*a* is to the left of *b*'; $\begin{smallmatrix}'a'\\b\end{smallmatrix}$ would mean '*a* is on top of *b*', and so on. A perfectly adequate symbolism, yet it has nothing corresponding to the '*R*' and '*S*'. This does not show that a symbolism which uses '*R*' and '*S*' is incorrect; but it does show that '*R*' and '*S*' are unnecessary, that they are part of the component in a proposition that has to do with the arrangement of the fact, and that an arrangement of names would do the job just as well. This, I think, is what Wittgenstein means by calling '*φx*' and '*xRy*' forms. They are forms, because they have to do with the arrangements, the forms of the facts; they pick out nothing material in the world. Consequently, they are not one of the ingredients of a proposition, but part of that structural side which make propositions into assertions.

But can this be what he means? He never says as much, and the biggest difficulty is with subject-predicate propositions. How could the '*φ*' in '*φa*' have to do with the arrangement of the object named by '*a*'? How can one object be *arranged*? But this is getting back to the problem in the *Tractatus* I began with. Does the state of affairs corresponding to '*φa*' contain only one object? Is '*φ*', after all, a name? Since there is little else in the pre-*Tractatus* material to help settle this difficulty, I shall have to leave it until I come to the *Tractatus*.

# III

# THE DOCTRINE OF SHOWING

## 1. *Introductory*

WITTGENSTEIN writes in the *Tractatus*:[1]

Propositions can represent the whole of reality, but they cannot represent what they must have in common with reality in order to be able to represent it—logical form.

Propositions cannot represent logical form: it is mirrored in them. . . . Propositions *show* the logical form of reality.

What *can* be shown, *cannot* be said.

These are the central theses in what has been called 'the Doctrine of Showing'. The Doctrine of Showing must be one of the most difficult parts of this difficult book; with few changes it reappears as the 'mysticism' at the close of the *Tractatus*,[2] and this is, if anything, even more difficult. Yet it is not easy to ignore; we have Wittgenstein reminding us, more than once, that he considers it the *main* point of the *Tractatus*. While he was still in prison camp, he managed to get a manuscript of the *Tractatus* to Russell, to which Russell responded, not surprisingly, with a list of questions. In his next letter to Russell, Wittgenstein at first begged off answering any of the questions specifically and contented himself with the general reply:[3]

Now I'm afraid that you haven't really got hold of my main contention to which the whole business of logical propositions is only corollary. The main point is the theory of what can be expressed (*gesagt*) by propositions, i.e. by language (and, which comes to the same thing, what can be thought) and what cannot be expressed by propositions, but only shown (*gezeigt*); which I believe is the cardinal problem of philosophy.

This last, rather startling remark was not a piece of epistolary intemperance on Wittgenstein's part, because much the same claim is made in the Preface to the *Tractatus*. The whole sense of the book, he says there:

[1] 4.12a; 4.121a, d; 4.1212.     [2] See esp. 6.522.
[3] Letter 18: Cassino, 19.8.19.

... might be summed up in the following words: what can be said at all can be said clearly, and what we cannot talk about we must consign to silence.

Fortunately, the considerations which led Wittgenstein to the Doctrine of Showing are to be found in the pre-*Tractatus* writings, and, as would be expected, its genesis reveals a geat deal about its meaning. The Doctrine of Showing, it turns out, is in part a development of Frege's *Grundgesetze* ideas on the definition of concepts, in part a reaction to Russell's Theory of Types, and in part the result of Wittgenstein's own thinking about the unique character of the propositions of logic.

## 2. *Its Genesis in the Pre-*Tractatus *Writings*

The Theory of Types, as was noticed early in the life of the theory, seemed to lead to two incompatible states of affairs. First, it required that the hierarchical order of types be strictly observed; a type of order $n$, according to the theory, should have as arguments only types of order $n-1$ and should be an argument for only types of order $n+1$. Now, several functions are, on this standard, ambiguous as to type: functions, namely, which can take arguments of several or all different orders. Such functions, because they do not behave as the Theory of Types requires, are improper; they can lead to contradiction and paradox; and what one tries to say with them, if there is any sense to it at all, must be expressed in a different way. (Wittgenstein, incidentally, has a good way of putting this; he says in the *Notebooks* that they are all on the Index.)[1] Then, secondly, the Theory of Types made words like 'thing', 'property', 'relation', 'fact', 'type', &c., important in logical vocabulary. So, the incompatibility is between, on the one hand, the theory's restriction on the behaviour of functions and, on the other, the vocabulary which the theory itself makes important. The items in the vocabulary do not themselves meet the requirement. 'Type', for example, can take an argument of any order; 'function' can take an argument of any order except the first; &c. Each is typically ambiguous. However, Wittgenstein did not think that this incompatibility called for revision in the

---

[1] *Nbk.* 8.10.14b.

Theory of Types. He thought, as we see in the *Notes Dictated to Moore*, that, much to the contrary, it shows a *theory* of types to be altogether impossible.[1] To *say* something like 'M is a thing' uses the typically ambiguous word 'thing'. To *say* that there are types or that a function can have as an argument only a type of an immediately lower order makes use of the typically ambiguous words 'type', 'function', and 'argument'. And these statements are what would make up a *theory* of types. But this does not leave logic in a difficult position, Wittgenstein says, because even were a theory of types possible, it is unnecessary:[2]

Even if there *were* propositions of [the] form 'M is a thing', they would be superfluous (tautologous) because what this tries to say is something which is already *seen* when you see 'M'.

So, a theory of types is both impossible and superfluous. First, what it tries to say cannot be said; second, what it tries to say is already *shown* by the symbolism. In order to say about a certain symbol what the Theory of Types wants to say, one would first have to know what the symbol is, and in knowing this one would *see* the type.[3]

How much, then, does one *see* in the symbolism? Or, in *Tractatus* terms, what *shows*? First, the nature of *M* shows:[4]

That M is a *thing* can't be *said*; it is nonsense: but *something* is *shown* by the symbol 'M'.

Also, the form of propositions shows:[5]

. . . that a *proposition* is a subject-predicate proposition can't be said: but it is *shown* by the symbol.

And, more generally:[6]

Every *real* proposition *shows* something, besides what it says, about the Universe: *for*, if it has no sense, it can't be used; and if it has a sense, it mirrors some logical property of the Universe.

This last passage is less clear as it stands than the other two, so I will add a little about it. Just as only certain types of elements in the world can fit together to make a fact, so only certain types of

---

[1] *NM* 108.33 *et seq.*     [2] *NM* 109.7–10.     [3] *NM* 109.17–21.
[4] *NM* 108.29–31.     [5] *NM* 108.31–32.     [6] *NM* 107.26–28.

symbols can combine to make propositions. In this sense, propositions *show* (mirror) the logical properties of the world. This, at any rate, is what I take to be the point here. And, in what appears to be elaboration of this point, Wittgenstein says that a language which did not mirror these properties, i.e. an illogical language, would be one in which 'you could put an *event* into a hole'.[1] In other words, there are different types of elements in the world, and we see that there are different types because we see that the elements of the world have different possibilities of combination with the other elements to make facts. Language too, has types, and they are determined in an analogous way, because language mirrors the behaviour as regards combining, i.e. mirrors the logical properties, of the world.

These remarks should suggest something about the still deeper foundations of Wittgenstein's Doctrine of Showing. The Theory of Types began as an attempt to solve problems presented by what Russell and Whitehead called 'illegitimate totalities', totalities in paradoxical propositions like 'All Cretans are liars', 'All generalizations are false', &c. Totalities are legitimate, Russell decided, only when all the members of the totality fall within the range of significance of some one function.[2] This means that we can speak of *all* of the members of some group only if the group forms part or the whole of the range of significance of some propositional function, where 'the range of significance' is defined by Russell as 'the collection of those arguments for which the function in question is significant, i.e. has a value.'[3] Then, 'types' come in via the notion of 'range of significance', in the following way:[4]

A *type* is defined as the range of significance of a propositional function, i.e., as the collection of arguments for which the said function has values. . . . Thus whatever contains an apparent variable must be of a different type from the possible values of that variable; we will say that it is of a *higher* type.

This is where the Doctrine of Showing reveals the *Grundgesetze* part of its ancestry. Types coincide with 'ranges of significance'.

[1] *NM* 107.6–9, 107.14–15.
[2] Russell: 'Mathematical Logic as Based on the Theory of Types', p. 74.
[3] Ibid., p. 75.          [4] Ibid., p. 75.

And 'range of significance' is the same thing as 'range of applicability', a phrase I used to interpret Wittgenstein's version of Frege's demand for completeness in definition. Briefly, Wittgenstein's version was: to know the sense of a symbol is to know, from the time it is introduced, all its possible combinations, i.e. its range of applicability. And, to repeat, the range in which a symbol is applicable is the range in which it is significant; these are the same thing. Therefore, Wittgenstein might well not accept the idea of a *theory* of types. Since one already knows the range of applicability of a symbol just by understanding it, and since the same must hold for the range of significance of the symbol, then one already knows what type of symbol it is. So, the type of a symbol is not a piece of knowledge we must discover about it in addition to understanding its sense. Any talk about types, given Wittgenstein's account of the sense of symbols, must be superfluous.

The third ancestor I said one finds in tracing the genealogy of the Doctrine of Showing is Wittgenstein's own reflection on the unique character of logical propositions. Logical propositions are not like ordinary ones in at least these respects. Ordinary propositions (i) say something about the world, and (ii) must therefore be checked with something in the world to determine their truth or falsity. Logical propositions need not be checked against the world, so cannot be saying anything about the world, at least in the sense in which the ordinary ones do. So, Wittgenstein begins with this distinction between logical and, as he calls them, real propositions.[1] But then the question arises: what is it that gives logical propositions their informative value? And Wittgenstein's answer is: logical propositions *show* something about the world; simply by looking at the symbol one sees certain 'properties' of the world.[2] Which properties? To use Wittgenstein's example,[3] consider the real propositions '$\phi a$', '$\phi a \supset \psi a$', and '$\psi a$', which form the tautology '$[\phi a. (\phi a \supset \psi a)] \supset (\psi a)$'. A real proposition, as we saw a short while ago in connexion with types, shows something about the fact corresponding to it. Each constituent real proposition in this tautology has a certain property; what the

---

[1] *NM* 107.1–5; see also 107.32, 108.17–19.    [2] *NM* 107.3–4.    [3] *NM* 107.29.

tautology as a whole does, Wittgenstein says, is to show 'in a systematic way' what these properties of the propositions are.[1] In this case it shows that, given the truth of '$\phi a$' and of '$\phi a \supset \psi a$', the truth of '$\psi a$' must follow. Thus, in general, tautologies show one of the important sorts of relations holding between real propositions; tautologies show that certain symbols must be true if certain others are.[2] So, again we are led to a Doctrine of Showing. There is more to language than saying that such and such is the case. Language shows; we understand things both about a symbolism and the Universe it mirrors just by looking at it.

### 3. *Its Position in the* Tractatus

For completeness's sake I must eventually describe the last stage of the genesis: how these ideas from the pre-*Tractatus* writings are modified in coming over into the *Tractatus*. Most of this I shall do when discussing the picture theory. I do want now, though, to explain where to look in the *Tractatus* for the Doctrine of Showing, because its most important appearances are by no means its most obvious. I shall do this by tracing the use of the words 'form' and 'formal' through the *Tractatus*, not in all their appearances but in those from which most of the rest seem to derive. As you will see, the words 'form' and 'formal' cover much the same ground in the *Tractatus* as we have so far covered in this genetic account of the Doctrine of Showing. The main discussion of the Doctrine of Showing appears in the 4.12's, and it is here too that we find the most extended use of the words 'form' and 'formal'. In a certain sense, Wittgenstein says, we can speak of the 'formal properties' of objects and of states of affairs, and in the same sense of 'formal relations'.[3] There is, of course, close connexion between the Doctrine of Showing and these so-called formal properties and relations; in fact, the Doctrine of Showing can be expressed in this way: what can be said in language is that this object has this *real* property or stands in this *real* relation to another object; what cannot be said is anything about the *formal* properties of objects or of states of affairs or about their *formal* relations; formal properties and relations show themselves. Then,

---

[1] *NM* 107.16–18.          [2] *NM* 108.23–24.          [3] 4.122a.

there is the related phrase 'formal concept'; formal concepts are those corresponding to formal properties.[1] Since the formal properties of objects and states of affairs cannot be expressed in language, formal concepts cannot be used; they are pseudo-concepts.[2] The point I want to make about this use of 'form' and 'formal' is that the examples Wittgenstein gives of formal concepts (viz. 'object', 'thing', 'fact', 'function', &c.)[3] are identical with the most obvious examples of typically ambiguous concepts in the Theory of Types; formal concepts are clearly the ones on the Index. And all of this discussion in the *Tractatus* can profitably be read as Wittgenstein's own Theory of Types (only, he insists, it is not a *theory*). It is true, Wittgenstein's version goes, that in a sense there are formal properties and relations and concepts, and it is true that they are different from first level or real properties, relations, and concepts. But it is wrong to think, say in the case of formal concepts, that the difference is just that they are on a higher level in the same hierarchy of concepts. They are pseudo-concepts; they cannot be used in language, and what they try to *say* instead *shows* in the symbolism.

Now, if we trace the words 'form' and 'formal' from their central use in the 4.12's back to their earlier uses, we come upon the phrases 'logical form' ('logische Form')[4] and 'pictorial form' ('Form der Abbildung').[5] The latter is a form of one kind of fact, viz. a picture, and it is defined as the possibility of the picture's structure. Then, tracing the words back further, the next earlier use is in the phrase 'the form of a state of affairs' ('die Form des Sachverhaltes').[6] Here the definition is: the form of a state of affairs is the possibility of its structure. The language in both these definitions brings us back to, and seems to derive from, the earliest appearance of the word 'form' in the *Tractatus*, the 'form of an object'.[7] The form of an object is, by definition, the possibility of its occurrence in states of affairs. In the terminology of the 4.12's, if we refer to the formal property of some object, we mean that object's possibility of occurrence in states of affairs. And we

[1] 4.126a.     [2] 4.126b, c; 4.1272a.     [3] 4.1272 *passim*.
[4] 2.18.     [5] 2.15; see also 2.151, 2.17.     [6] 2.033.
[7] 2.0141; see also 2.0233, 2.0251.

can see from the explanation of what it is to know an object,[1] that knowing the *form* of an object is not something different from simply knowing the object; these are not two items of knowledge, but one.

This is a sketchy job,[2] but all I want to demonstrate with it is that in tracing the words 'form' and 'formal' we are led from, at the start, considerations about knowing what an object is which are strongly reminiscent of Wittgenstein's version of Frege's demand for completeness in symbols, to, at the end, an alternative version of Russell's Theory of Types, and all of this within the framework of the *Tractatus* Doctrine of Showing. So, the route which led *to* the Doctrine of Showing is all of it still there *in* the Doctrine of Showing, worked out in detail and with some indication of its unity in the recurrence of the words 'form' and 'formal'. And I might add that, as this brief sketch makes plain, the Doctrine of Showing is not confined simply to the distinction in the 4.12's between saying and showing. This is important because, when one sees how much it includes, one may be able to see better why Wittgenstein considered it the *main* point of the *Tractatus*.

[1] 2.0123a.

[2] Some of the many appearances of 'form' and 'formal' not considered are: 2.023 the unalterable form of the world (also 2.026), 2.025 substance is form and content, 2.173 *Form der Darstellung* (also 2.174), 3.13e form of the sense of a proposition, 3.31d expressions are marks of form and content, 4.1252a formal series (also 4.1273, 5.252, 5.2522, 5.501 ff.), 4.5 most general propositional form (also 4.53, 5.46 ff., 5.47 ff., 6, 6.01), 5.501 ff. formal law, 6 form of a truth function, 6.022 general form of a number (also 6.03), 6.32 law of causality is the form of a law.

# IV

# FROM ATOMIC TO MOLECULAR PROPOSITIONS

I WANT to say something about the rest of the pre-*Tractatus* theories: not in detail, only enough to place atomic propositions in their context.

What is an atomic proposition? It is a proposition all of whose components are indefinables and containing no logical constants. This is clear from *Notes on Logic*[1] and is stated explicitly in *Notes Dictated to Moore*.[2] Now, at this time Wittgenstein believed that there were several kinds of atomic propositions: subject-predicate, dyadic relational, triadic relational, &c.;[3] so, atomic propositions have the same *form*, at least, as propositions with which we are familiar. As one could guess from the theory of indefinables, it is only atomic propositions which have contact with the world; or, to use Wittgenstein's phrase, atomic propositions have all the 'material information' to be found in language.[4] And in as much as the sense of a function of '$p$' is a function of the sense of '$p$'[5] and molecular propositions are, by definition, functions of atomic propositions, it is atomic propositions that are the primary bearers of sense; molecular propositions have a sense in virtue of the atomic propositions they contain.

Molecular propositions are, by definition, truth-functions of the atomic ones. Thus, what is essential to a molecular proposition is a true-false schema, a statement of the cases for which the proposition is true and the cases for which it is false.[6] Now, it is possible to produce *all* functions and so *all* molecular propositions by performing a single operation repeatedly on atomic propositions, as Sheffer demonstrated:[7]

If now we find an *ab* [i.e. *true-false*] function of such a kind that by repeated applications of it every *ab*-function can be generated, then we

---

[1] See Ch. II.1–2.    [2] *NM* 110.35–36.
[3] *NL* VI 12–17; see also VI 37–40.    [4] *NL* III 1–5, 7–9; cf. *LF* p. 163.
[5] *NL* I 164–5 and III 63.    [6] *NL* III 5–7.
[7] *NL* III 104–8; see also III 80–95.

can introduce the totality of $ab$-functions as the totality of those that are generated by the application of this function. Such a function is $\sim p \vee \sim q$.

These are, in very general terms, the features of atomic and molecular propositions. Confronted with a molecular proposition one should, in theory, in something of a reversal of Sheffer's operation, be able to reduce it to its constituent propositions by analysis. Wittgenstein does not put it quite like this; what he says is:[1]

Every statement about complexes can be resolved into the logical sum of a statement about the constituents and a statement about the proposition which describes the complex completely.

Now, the operation described here obviously breaks up complexes into their constituents, and I assume that he means that this same operation will reduce *all* complexes to their *ultimate* constituents, that this single operation is the only one necessary to reduce to atomic constituents. If this is right, then analysis is an important subject for study. To understand it would be to understand in more concrete terms what the fully analysed (i.e. atomic) proposition is like, especially in its relation to ordinary language. But these are complicated matters, and I want to leave analysis and its ramifications until they come up again, in greater detail, in the *Tractatus*.

There is, though, one final piece of information in the pre-*Tractatus* writings I shall mention. In *Notes Dictated to Moore* Wittgenstein again takes up the question of what symbolizes in '*aRb*'. He expresses some doubt about the explanation he had given previously.[2] He had said previously that what symbolizes is that '*R*' comes between '*a*' and '*b*'. But he now remarks that the symbols '*a*', '*R*', and '*b*' are not simple; the proposition '*aRb*' is analysable. So how can we be confident that this explanation really explains much about language—that is, about propositions of the form '*aRb*'? But, says Wittgenstein in response:

... what seems certain is that when we have analysed it we shall in the end come to propositions of the same form in respect of the fact that they do consist in one thing being between two others.

[1] *NL* II 69–71; see also II 72–78.　　[2] *NM* 110.20–26.

This way of talking suggests that atomic propositions are far removed from propositions of ordinary language. Then, later in the *Notes Dictated to Moore*, Wittgenstein speaks of 'the general form of a proposition'. Again, he voices some hesitation:[1] how is it possible to talk about the general form of *all* propositions when there is a whole class, viz. 'unanalysable propositions in which particular names and relations occur', with which we are not even acquainted? He says in response:

What justifies us in doing this is that though we don't know any unanalysable propositions of this kind, yet we can understand what is meant by a proposition of the form $(\exists x, y, R)$. $xRy$ (which is unanalysable), even though we know no proposition of the form $xRy$.

This, of course, is not limited to atomic propositions of the form '$xRy$'; the implication is that we are not acquainted with any atomic propositions at all. So, at this time were Wittgenstein asked what atomic propositions were like, he would be willing to give at least this negative information: we can eliminate from consideration any proposition, no matter how simple, of ordinary language.

[1] *NM* 110.27–33.

# V

# THE WORLD

## 1. *Introductory*

IT is obvious how, at least in general terms, to describe the subject of the *Tractatus*: the *Tractatus* is about the relation between language and the world. With the addition of one or two notes this description, general as it is, is a good guide to the early parts of the *Tractatus*. First, for 'world' we should understand 'any world'. When Wittgenstein says in the 1's that 'the world is all that is the case' or that 'the world divides into facts', this is not intended as a truth about the world as in fact it is. He does sometimes speak of 'the world' meaning 'the world as in fact it is' but only to say, in effect, that describing 'the world' in this sense is not his business.[1] Similarly, for 'language' we must read 'any language'. Wittgenstein's interest is not in features which, as a matter of fact, some languages possess, but in features which, as a matter of logic, all languages must possess.[2]

Now, the first subject of the *Tractatus*, the subject of the 1's, is the world as a whole. This short, schematic account starts by saying that the world is all that is the case, the totality of facts ('Tatsachen'), and it ends by saying that the world divides into unit-facts, facts which are the end points in the reduction of complex facts to their constituents. A unit-fact, it becomes clear, is the existence of a state of affairs ('Sachverhalt'). And the first section of the 2's, the 2.0's, examines these states of affairs in detail. Then, the second section of the 2's, the 2.1's, introduces language, language in the widest sense. We make pictures of facts; in the first instance what we picture are these unit-facts, i.e. these existent states of affairs. Then, the third and final section of the 2's, the 2.2's, is about the relation between facts and pictures. First, picture and fact have logical form in common; second, the picture contains the possibility of the situation it pictures; third, the picture can either agree with the fact or not, and in this agreement or disagreement its truth or falsity consists. So, we

[1] 5.551; see also 2.0121c, 6.1233.    [2] See 4.5b, 5.471, 5.4711.

have in the 1's and 2's a straightforward, though quite abstract, statement of what the world (any world) must be like, what language (any language) must be like, and what relations must hold between them. Wittgenstein is, of course, still occupied with these subjects after the 1's and 2's, but his interests quickly become more special. Early in the 3's he abandons language in the wide sense and takes it up in the more familiar sense of sentences ('Sätze') and words.[1] So, the 1's and 2's remain Wittgenstein's statement, at its most complete and freest from the distractions of special cases, of the relation between language and the world.

This chapter is about the 1's. And I leave argumentation for what I claim here till later chapters; for now I content myself with the sufficiently difficult task of trying to state clearly what the 1's say.

## 2. *The World as the Totality of Facts*

The 1's begin: the world is all that is the case, the totality of facts and not of things.[2] Without giving any of these words technical senses they later acquire in the *Tractatus*, I think one would interpret this statement as follows. Facts are generically different from things; facts have things as constituents; but they are not just the set of these things; they are these things plus configuration. Though this is obvious, we tend to forget it and to 'objectify' facts. Take this room, for example: it is not, as we tend to think, just this desk, these chairs, this lamp, and so on. It is different in kind; it is these things *with some arrangement, standing in some relation to one another*. Similarly with the world; it is the totality, not of things, but of facts. Now, I think that certainly Wittgenstein means this much in 1 and 1.1, but I think that he also intends us to take the words in their technical senses, whether or not they have yet been introduced. It is not novel to suggest that the propositions of the *Tractatus* can be read in two ways: either in the order in which they appear on the page, or in the order of their 'logical importance'.[3] That is, instead of going from 1 to 1.1 to 1.11 and

---

[1] 3.1, 3.14.
[2] 1, 1.1; cf. Russell: *Our Knowledge of the External World*, pp. 60 *et seq.*
[3] For this expression, see Wittgenstein's note to 1.

so on, it is one of the intentions of the numbering system that we also go from 1 to 2 to 3 and so on. Reading this second way, then, we go from 'the world is all that is the case' (1) to 'what is the case —a fact—is the existence of states of affairs' (2), and obviously the phrase 'what is the case' in 1 is to be understood in light of the explanation in 2. By parity of reasoning, as with the expression 'what is the case' so with the word 'thing'. In 1.1 'thing' already bears the technical sense it is later given. A 'thing' is the same as an 'object',[1] and 'object', we know, has a very special meaning in the *Tractatus*. Indeed, in the early parts of the *Tractatus* the word 'thing' is used with this special meaning as least as frequently as is the word 'object'.[2]

So, we may also interpret 1 and 1.1 in the following way. The world is not just things; we would not characterize the world by listing objects. We would not, I think, because, as we are told later, objects are unalterable: they are unalterable both in the sense that they remain the same through change[3] and in the sense that they are present in any possible world.[4] That is, no matter what changes we imagine something's going through, the objects involved are what have not changed; and no matter how we imagine the world as different from what it is, the objects will be common both to this and the imagined world. If being unalterable in this sense is a necessary condition of being an object, then of course it is of no help in characterizing a world to list the objects. Such lists would be identical for all possible worlds, so nothing characteristic could be given by them.

What are objects like? Can one give examples? In the *Notebooks* Wittgenstein does seem to have a fairly concrete picture in mind when he speaks of objects. They are what is simple, what cannot be subdivided.[5] So, the material bodies we meet with in every day life, being capable of subdivision, are not objects. Wittgenstein then asks himself:[6]

Is spatial complexity also logical complexity?

to which he answers:

---

[1] 2.01.      [2] See 2.011, 2.012, 2.0121a–b, 2.0122, 2.013, &c.      [3] 2.0271.
[4] 2.022, 2.023.      [5] *Nbk.* 25.4.15d, 13.5.15d, 23.5.15e, 14.6.15c, 17.6.15i, &c.
[6] *Nbk.* 7.5.15a; see also 17.6.15f.

It surely seems to be.

And later he answers more emphatically:[1]

The division of the body into *material points*, as we have it in physics, is nothing more than analysis into *simple components*.

Material bodies are things like books,[2] watches,[3] &c. They are not objects, because a watch, for instance, is made up of component parts, e.g. wheels.[4] Obviously the wheels cannot be objects either, because we can divide them into components parts. However, if we go on in this way, we eventually reach components which themselves do not have components. These simples, which are of interest to logic, are like material points, which are of interest to physics.

If we now explore the picture suggested by the *Notebooks*, we can perhaps see in it grounds for the belief that objects are unalterable and that facts, not objects, constitute the world. Wittgenstein says that objects are both (i) unchanging and (ii) common to all possible worlds. (i) Material points are unchanging in just the way physicists have long said. Change is always change in the configuration of these points; the points themselves never change; they only group and re-group. And (ii) material points will be seen to be common to all possible worlds, once we observe that all we can do in imagination is invent new arrangements of these simple elements; again, all that can vary is the pattern, never the elements themselves. Then, Wittgenstein says that the world is the sum of facts, not of objects. If material points are objects, then it is true that one can characterize the world only by saying that objects have some configuration. The world consists of watch-wheels, watches, books, &c. These are not objects but objects plus configuration. In other words, they are facts: the facts *that* such and such objects stand in such and such relations to one another.

This brings us to the next part of the 1's: the world is determined by facts and by their being *all* facts, because the sum of facts determines both what is the case and what is not the case.[5] The world is composed of facts, and facts are configurations of

---

[1] *Nbk.* 20.6.15m; see also 21.6.15f.     [2] *Nbk.* 23.5.15f, 20.6.15 o *et seq.*
[3] *Nbk.* 16.6.15a *et seq.*          [4] *Nbk.* 18.6.15i.     [5] 1.11, 1.12.

objects. Clearly facts can be of different degrees of complexity. This watch-wheel, being a configuration of certain objects, is a fact in its own right. Yet the watch itself is a still more complex fact and, in some sense, includes this other fact. Then, this watch, say, stands to the left of this book, which in turn is on top of this table. If we go on with this long enough, we will soon reach the level of complexity of this room. And there is nothing to prevent our going on until we reach the level of the world. Thus, we can generalize: objects by themselves determine nothing about a world; complexes do determine some features of the world; the larger the complex the more features will be determined; until finally, the arrangement of all objects having been specified, the world is fully determined. So, this is how the word 'determined' ('bestimmt') in 'the world is determined by facts' is to be understood. Then there is the added point: the world is so determined, because the sum of facts determines both what is the case and what is not the case. To determine one arrangement for a group of objects, I take Wittgenstein to be saying here, is also to determine that those objects do not have any other arrangement.

The next part[1] of the 1's says: the world divides into facts, and any unit can either be the case or not the case and all the rest remain unaffected.[2] It is easy to see one of Wittgenstein's reasons for holding this. The world is determined by all the facts, that is, by these objects configured in this way and forming this fact, which fact is part of a more complex fact, which in turn is part of a still more complex fact, and so on. If this is the very rough picture of the world Wittgenstein has so far given us, the converse will hold as well. The world can be divided into complex facts and simpler facts; just as this room, say, is built up out of facts, it can be divided into facts. Now, how far can this division go? We know that the opposite process is finished when all objects have some configuration, i.e. when a world is completely determined. When is division finished?

This is the question 1.21 goes on to answer, but what the

---

[1] I omit 1.13, which says 'The facts in logical space are the world'; I consider this metaphor later (Ch. VIII.5).
[2] 1.2, 1.21.

answer is takes more than the usual amount of explaining. 1.21 presents a vexing linguistic difficulty.[1] A natural translation for the word 'eines' in 1.21 would be something like 'any one', which would make the passage read:

1.2 The world divides into facts.
1.21 Any one can be the case or not the case and all the rest remain unaffected.

This, of course, suggests that the 'any one' is any one of the facts mentioned immediately before in 1.2. But this cannot be right. 'Eines', being neuter, is not referring to the feminine 'Tatsachen'; nor, if we then look in the opposite direction, can it be referring to the masculine 'Sachverhalte' in 2. Apparently it does not refer outside itself at all, and perhaps the meaning of 1.21 would best be conveyed by some such gloss as:

Any one of the kind of thing that can be the case can be the case or not while the rest of them remain unaffected.

There is a parallel to 'eines' in the 'alles' in 1, and the parallel gloss is probably appropriate there too:

The world is all the things of the kind that can be the case that are the case.

If so, then the *eines* in 1.21 is *one* of the sort of thing of which *all* are mentioned in 1, viz. the sort of thing that can be the case. And what are they? They are, I believe, states of affairs; as, I think, either of the following arguments shows. First compare propositions 1 and 2. 1 says: the world is all that is the case; and 2 says: what is the case, i.e. a fact, is the existence of states of affairs. 2 is intended, I think, as a statement about the general features of the world, in the following sense. It says that what is the case, from the general point of view, is the existence of states of affairs. Thus, when 1 says that the world is all that is the case, this is to say that the world is all existent states of affairs; and when 1.1 adds that the world is the totality of facts, this, again, is to say that the world is the totality of existent states of affairs. This is

[1] Cf. the Ogden with the Pears and McGuinness translation; this difficulty was brought to my attention by Pears and McGuinness in a class they gave in Oxford.

good, though not yet conclusive, evidence that 'all the things that
are the case' is equivalent to 'the sum of existent states of affairs'
and thus that 'a thing that is the case' is equivalent to 'an existent
state of affairs'. And these equivalences strongly suggest that
'existing' and 'being the case' are different ways of saying the same
thing, and that in each case the subject of the verb is a 'state of
affairs'. The fact that 'eines' in 1.21 cannot be referring to 'Sachverhalte' in 2 would not, I think, count against this interpretation;
my gloss shows a way of reading 1.21 which leaves open the
possibility that the sort of thing spoken of might be specified later.
A second route to the same conclusion is this. The most apparent
candidates for the position of the kind of thing that can be the
case are facts and states of affairs. As for facts, it is hard to see
what a fact's being or not being the case could mean. I do not see
any special interpretation of Wittgenstein's 'facts' that would
make it intelligible to say of them both that they are not the case
and that they are still facts. In contrast to this, states of affairs,
we know, can exist or not.[1] Being only possible, we can say of them
that they are or are not the case, or that they do or do not exist.
So, of the two, states of affairs is the more likely candidate, and
barring the appearance of another it would have to be accepted.

From these considerations we can derive a final gloss of 1.21:

Any one state of affairs can either be the case or not and all other states
of affairs remain unaffected.

We know by the numbering that this is a comment on 1.2's claim
that the world divides into facts. For convenience I shall call the
property which 1.21 attributes to states of affairs their 'existential
independence'. Suppose from two states of affairs, $A$ and $B$,
we construct the logical product $A.B$. Now, it certainly cannot be
said of this product that it is existentially independent; it could
not exist if either $A$ or $B$ did not exist. Therefore, when Wittgenstein says that states of affairs are existentially independent, what
he means by states of affairs cannot be complex; they cannot, in
other words, be capable of division into simpler states of affairs.
This now shows us how existential independence (the subject of

[1] 2.06–2.062.

1.21) is connected with division (the subject of 1.2): that states of affairs are existentially independent means that they are simple. Since this remark comes right after we are told that the world divides into facts, this suggests that division has an end, that states of affairs are *the* simples.

### 3. *'The World' and 'Reality'*

Almost no matter how one interprets these remarks about 'the world', a dilemma arises. Wittgenstein says implicitly in the *Tractatus*[1] and explicitly in a letter to Russell[2] that elementary propositions are always positive. He also says in this letter,[3] and in the *Tractatus* as well,[4] that a state of affairs is what corresponds to an elementary proposition when it is true. From this it follows that states of affairs are always positive. Now, states of affairs are the sort of things that are the case. Thus, since the world is all that is the case,[5] the world is all existent states of affairs. But the world is also the sum of facts.[6] Therefore, facts must be the same as existent states of affairs. Then, since states of affairs are positive, so must facts be. So, the world is the sum of facts (positive facts). However, when we turn to the last few propositions of the 2.0's, the impression they give is quite different. 2.06 introduces the word 'reality', and reality, we are told, is the existence and non-existence of states of affairs. The existence of a state of affairs is a positive fact, and the non-existence a negative fact. Therefore reality includes both positive and negative facts. Now, this in itself creates no troubles. We could say that Wittgenstein uses two terms, 'the world' and 'reality'; the first he uses to refer to the sum of positive facts only and the second to refer to the sum of positive and negative facts; 'reality', in other words, is the more inclusive term. But trouble comes at 2.063, where Wittgenstein says that the sum-total of reality is the world. The equation, evidently, is complete. The word 'sum-total' ('gesamt') does not leave even a small possibility that reality might be wider than the world. Thus, the world, as the sum-total of reality, is the sum of facts (both positive and negative facts).

---

[1] See esp. 4.211.       [2] Letter 18: Cassino, 19.8.19, para. 6.
[3] Ibid., para. 1.       [4] 4.25.       [5] 1.       [6] 1.1.

We can treat this contradiction as a slip. We can say that in equating reality with the world in the 2.0's, Wittgenstein forgot that he said things in the 1's which restricted the world to positive facts. But his memory would have to be shorter than this; at 2.04 he again says (this time yet more straightforwardly than in the 1's) that the world is the sum of existent states of affairs, i.e. positive facts. Only one proposition separates this repetition of his original idea of the world and his definition of reality. His memory is unlikely to be that short; what is more probable, I think, is that he does wish to say at the same time: (i) the world is the sum of existent states of affairs, (ii) reality includes positive and negative facts, and (iii) reality = the world. Now, assuming that no slip is involved, if we look back at the 1's, we can perhaps see signs that much of this is already said there. 1.11 says that the world is determined by facts, and 1.21 explains that this is so *because* the sum of facts determines both what is the case and what is not the case. Does this not imply that the world therefore must be both what is the case and what is not the case, and thus that it includes both positive and negative facts? Of course, this would get rid of the conflict *between* the 1's and 2.0's by placing it *inside* each, and these three claims of Wittgenstein's would have still to be reconciled. I can see one way to reconcile them, but evidence is so scarce that whether or not it is Wittgenstein's way is difficult to tell. Negative facts are mentioned in the *Tractatus*, in all, only three times: besides 2.06b, at 4.063a and again at 5.5151a. The only other information we get, and this not by name, is at 1.12 and 2.05. And though these propositions are compatible with, may even be thought to suggest, the following solution, they do not do more than this.

Positive and negative facts differ in kind. Consider positive facts. The world is the sum of them, i.e. the sum of existent states of affairs. Of course, when we collect all existent states of affairs, we have the world; nothing need be added. Thus, the totality of positive facts is the whole world, and a single positive fact is one part of the world. Now, this is not the case with negative facts. If we add the whole set of negative facts to a group of positive facts, this is not at all like adding even one more positive fact. Negative facts are not part of the world, in the sense of 'part' I have used above. On the contrary, negative facts are such that once we have a set of positive facts we have a set of negative facts, as it were, automatically. In this sense we can speak of negative facts' being inseparable from positive facts. Thus, when Wittgenstein says that the world is the sum of positive facts, this may be taken to mean that the world is completely constituted by existent states of affairs. When he says that the world includes both positive and negative facts, this may be taken to refer to their inseparability; with a set of positive facts comes a set of negative facts. And since the world's being completely constituted by existent states of affairs and positive and negative facts' being inseparable do not rule one another out, Wittgenstein's three claims need not be incompatible.

# VI

# OBJECTS

## 1. Introductory

THE 2's have three main parts: the 2.0's, which are about those units, states of affairs, the existence of which constitutes the world; the 2.1's, which are about the pictures we make of the world; and the 2.2's, which are about the relation between the world and the pictures. I start now on the first of these three parts, the 2.0's. They, in turn, break up into four parts. The 2.01's present the first important characteristic of objects, namely, that an object is by essence a constituent of states of affairs. The 2.02's present their second important characteristic; objects are simple. The 2.03's add to objects the dimension of configuration; they describe how objects come together to form states of affairs. Finally, 2.04, 2.05, and the 2.06's add to objects and their configuration the dimension of existence; they discuss the existence and non-existence of states of affairs. In this section I take up the first two of these four parts, the two about objects.

## 2. Objects Are Constituents of States of Affairs

A state of affairs is a combination of objects.[1] And the thesis of the 2.01's is: not only do objects occur in states of affairs, they cannot not occur in them.[2] An object's possibility of occurrence in states of affairs is not, in the neologism Wittgenstein employs at 2.0121c, merely-possible ('nur-möglich').[3] Its occurrence in any one might be accidental, but the possibility of its occurrence in one or another is essential to it.[4] In support of this thesis Wittgenstein offers two arguments; others may perhaps be distinguished, but these are the important ones. The first is an indirect proof.

---

[1] 2.01.    [2] 2.011.

[3] Perhaps not Wittgenstein's coinage; see the distinction between 'Nurmöglichkeit' and 'Auchmöglichkeit' in A. Meinong: *Über Möglichkeit und Wahrscheinlichkeit*, esp. pp. 99–100. This earlier use was brought to my attention by Prof. G. Ryle.

[4] 2.0122.

DWLA

Suppose the appearance of objects in states of affairs were merely-possible. Then an object could as well exist alone as in a state of affairs. But if an object which existed alone on its own account subsequently occurred in a state of affairs, it would look like an accident that the state of affairs could be made to fit.[1] The point is that it never does look accidental. We know there is no chance about it because we know that the object just is the kind of thing that constitutes such states of affairs. Then, second, we see what is essential to objects in what is essential in being acquainted with them. If I know an object, Wittgenstein says, I thereby know all its possible occurrences in states of affairs.[2] Since this is essential to knowing the object, it must be essential to the object. Or, in the more traditional language into which Wittgenstein translates this point:[3]

If I am to know an object, though I need not know its external properties, I must know all its internal properties.

And its internal properties are its possibilities of occurrence in states of affairs.

The argument is simple, and how it connects with Wittgenstein's ideas on forms in *Notes on Logic*[4] and with his Doctrine of Showing[5] should be clear. But its very brevity produces questions, all of which it will be important eventually to answer. Is knowing the form of an object a sufficient or only a necessary condition for knowing the object? I think that it can only be necessary, because, as Wittgenstein tells us elsewhere,[6] there can be two or more objects with the same form, and consequently if in knowing the object I did not know more than the form, I would not know that two objects with the same form were not the same object. A second question is not so easily answered.[7] Wittgenstein says: if a thing can occur in a state of affairs, the possibility of the state of affairs must be written into the thing itself.[8] But does this mean: (i) if a thing can occur in a particular state of affairs, the possibility of that state of affairs must be written into it, or (ii) if a thing can

---

[1] 2.0121a.          [2] 2.0123a, c.          [3] 2.01231.          [4] See Ch. II.3–4.
[5] See Ch. III.2.          [6] 2.0233.
[7] It was brought to my attention by McGuinness and Pears in their class.
[8] 2.012.

occur in states of affairs, its possibility of occurring in, simply, states of affairs is written into it? Unfortunately, almost all the 2.01's can be read either way, but there is other evidence to assure us that no matter what Wittgenstein is saying at any one place in the 2.01's he does in the end hold the first, stronger position. At one point he considers the question: can we decide *a priori* whether there might not be a situation which had to be symbolized by a sign for a 27-termed relation?[1] Among other things, he says of this: we could never decide such a thing *a priori*, because we would first have to know what kinds (forms) of objects there were, and this is an empirical matter. So, it is not impossible for there to be objects capable of entering 27-termed relations; nor is it impossible for there to be objects which can enter only 2-termed relations. That is, the *Tractatus* allows that there might be (though, as an *a priori* study, it is not concerned with whether there are) objects of different forms. If there were, then to know these objects I should have to know their *different* forms; and their possibilities of occurrence in *particular* states of affairs would be written into them. Now, a third question arises out of settling this second one. Granted that objects might be of different forms, in what will the difference consist? There might be objects which can appear in 2-termed contexts alone; perhaps there are objects which can appear in either 2- or 3-termed contexts; and so on. Does the form then consist merely in the complexity of the context (or contexts) in which the object can appear? If it did, then we could indicate the form of an object merely by attaching a numerical subscript (or subscripts) to it.[2] If it is more than this, what more? At this point all I can do is raise the question; its answer largely depends on what in the end we decide objects are like.

### 3. *Analysis (1)*

The second characteristic of objects is that they are simple. This is the argument of the 2.02's, and it is the most important single

---

[1] 5.5541.
[2] This, again, I owe to McGuinness' and Pears' class, in particular to a suggestion by A. J. Kenny.

argument in the *Tractatus*. It reveals what analysis is, and by implication what the simples are like, and why there must be such simples, and that these simples constitute the substance of the world. And so much are these subjects at the centre of Wittgenstein's logical atomism that were the 2.02's understood well, most of the rest of the *Tractatus* would be clear. To the extent that they are not well understood, there are bound to be disagreements in interpretation of the *Tractatus* of the most elementary sort. One illustration of this is the disagreement over whether objects are particulars. There are those who say that objects must be particulars alone[1] and then those who say that, besides particulars, properties and relations are objects too.[2] I am going to spend a great deal of time on the propositions of the 2.02's, most of it on the single proposition, 2.0201. I do so both because they are so important and because there is practically no agreement about their meaning.

2.0201 says:

Every statement about complexes can be resolved into a statement about their constituents and into the propositions that describe the complexes completely.

A plausible way of reading this is to take its analysis as the analysis in Russell's Theory of Descriptions. So far as there is such a thing with the *Tractatus*, this is the usual interpretation. My general view on analysis is that the usual interpretation needs revision. So what I shall do is first state it, then argue that it fits the *Tractatus* poorly, then offer a new interpretation.

Take as an example of a statement about a complex the statement 'the book on the table is red'. On the usual interpretation this is to be analysed:

$$( \exists x) (Bx.Tx.(y) [(By.Ty) \supset (x=y)].Rx)$$

$Bx:$ '$x$ is a book'
$Tx:$ '$x$ is on the table'
$Rx:$ '$x$ is red'

---

[1] E.g. G. E. M. Anscombe: *An Introduction to Wittgenstein's Tractatus*, Ch. 7, esp. pp. 109 *et seq.*

[2] E.g. E. Stenius: *Wittgenstein's Tractatus: A Critical Exposition*, Ch. 5, esp. p. 63.

According to 2.0201 what we do in analysis is to resolve the statement about a complex into: (i) a statement about the constituents of the complex, and (ii) those propositions which describe the complex completely. Where do we find (i) and (ii) in the analysis above? Probably like this:

ii: $(\exists x)\ (Bx.Tx.(y)\ [(By.Ty) \supset (x=y)]$ . . .
i: . . . $Rx)$

What I have marked as (ii), that is, as the propositions which describe the complex completely, is fairly certain. In *Notes on Logic*, after describing analysis in nearly the terms he uses in the *Tractatus*,[1] Wittgenstein adds that the proposition which describes the complex completely is 'that proposition which is equivalent to saying the complex exists';[2] and in my example this must be the part of the analysis which says that there is some $x$ which is a book and is on the table. If this is right, then it leaves only '$Rx$'. So, '$Rx$' must be a 'statement about the constituents of the complex'. There is some difficulty in this. It is hard to see what sense can be attached to calling '$Rx$' a statement about the constituents of the complex. '$Rx$' is about $x$ (loosely speaking), and so evidently $x$ is the constituent(s) of the complex. The only sense I can make of this is that we might say that $x$ is a constituent in the sense that it is the *real* constituent of the complex. In other words, this would be to say that the real constituent of the complex *the book on the table* is the thing which is the book on the table. I am not sure how much sense this makes, but I do not see what else one could say.

In outline, then, this is the usual interpretation. And it seems to me not to fit the *Tractatus* at all well.

(1) The first thing, as we have seen, is that it does not comfortably fit the language of 2.0201.

(2) Then, supposedly the analysis that 2.0201 describes takes us all the way from complexes, no matter what the level of complexity, to simples.[3] Well, suppose we analyse the statement 'the book or the table is red' into:

---

[1] *NL* II 69–78.  [2] *NL* II 77–78.
[3] See esp. 3.201, 3.25, 3.3442, 4.221.

$$( \exists x)\ (Bx.Tx.Rx)$$

(for brevity I leave out the restriction '$(y)\ [(By.Ty) \supset (x = y)]$').
This new statement still involves, among other things, the predicate 'red', and we know that a statement making a colour attribution cannot be elementary.[1] So, we must analyse the predicate
'red'. But how do we do that? This kind of analysis does not seem
to be able to. It seems to consist, roughly speaking, in switching
a description from subject to predicate place and in introducing a
bound variable to serve as subject, and it seems not to involve any
means of reducing the descriptions themselves. Another way of
putting the same point is this. Since the analysis of 'the book on
the table is red' is:

$$( \exists x)\ (Bx.Tx.Rx)$$

and since this is not yet elementary, we must carry on with the
analysis. But how are we to re-apply this *same* method of analysis
to a proposition which is already in *this* form? Yet, obviously the
analysis has to go further.

(3) The early 3.2's tell us what a fully analysed proposition is
like. We can make propositions such that the elements of the
proposition correspond to the objects of the thought.[2] The objects
of the thought, since a thought is a picture of a fact,[3] correspond
to the objects in the fact which is being pictured.[4] From this it
follows that facts can be pictured in such a way that to the objects
of the fact correspond the elements of the propositional sign. Now,
the elements of such a propositional sign, since they stand for
objects,[5] are names.[6] And the configuration of the names in the
propositional sign corresponds to the configuration of the objects
in the fact.[7] Such a proposition is *fully analysed*.[8] Thus, a fully
analysed proposition is one with only names in some configuration. So if we are ever interested in the simplicity or complexity
of some proposition, we should ask: are the only signs in it names?
If so, it is fully analysed. As for the non-fully analysed proposition,
at 3.24b Wittgenstein remarks that a complex can be given in a
proposition only by its description. Thus, any proposition which
makes mention of a complex must also contain a description.

[1] 6.3751c.        [2] 3.2.        [3] 3.        [4] 2.13, 2.131.
[5] 3.22.        [6] 3.202.        [7] 3.21.        [8] 3.201; see also 4.22, 4.221.

Now, suppose it takes $n$ applications of analysis to reduce a given proposition to its fully analysed form. Then, after only $n-1$ applications we are still left with a proposition requiring analysis, a proposition making mention of a complex, and thus a proposition containing a description. Say it is the proposition '$fA$', where '$A$' is the description. Now, the final application of analysis—that is, on the usual interpretation—will be to translate the proposition '$fA$' into the form:

$$( \exists x) (Ax.fx)$$

And this must be fully analysed; there is nothing more to analyse, because this was the $n$-th translation. So, the propositional sign

$$( \exists x) (Ax.fx)$$

is fully analysed. But this does not meet any of the requirements. It is not just names in some configuration; it contains two functions. Furthermore, not only ought this not to contain non-names, it ought also to contain some names. But where are they? '$x$' is not a name but a bound variable, a distinction which in the *Tractatus* seems clearly marked.[1] And even taking '$x$' as a name, there are still difficulties. At 4.22 Wittgenstein says that an elementary proposition consists of names in some combination and that the analysis of propositions must eventually bring us to such elementary propositions. Then 4.23 says:

It is only in the nexus of an elementary proposition that a name occurs in a proposition.

This seems very much to imply that in analysis we shall meet names only upon reaching elementary propositions, that names appear only at the final stage of analysis. But on this interpretation of analysis an '$x$' does not appear only then; it is introduced as soon as analysis begins.

(4) Supposedly the proposition '$fA$' is analysed:

$$( \exists x) (Ax.fx)$$

But suppose '$A$' were a description like 'triangle'. Now, this itself can be broken down into elements. But this would be a new kind of reduction. I mean on the usual interpretation of 2.0201

[1] See 3.312b, 3.314b, 3.315, 4.1272a, 4.1273a, 5.526b, 5.5261.

the analysis of propositions does not include reduction of this sort. Yet it seems necessary in order to reach elementary propositions. And, more important, Wittgenstein seems to say that what he means by analysis includes this kind of reduction. At 3.24d he says that there are symbols, which, since they cannot be names, are probably descriptions, which are definable. At 3.261b he implies that one must keep on defining until one reaches primitive signs, and 3.261a would then say that all defined signs signify via those primitive signs which define them. At 3.26 Wittgenstein implies, by saying that names cannot be analysed further by definitions, that some signs can be and that the definition is a kind of analysis. One ought not to make too much out of these propositions alone. But it is striking that, if primitive signs are identical with names, then both analysis and definition are ways of reducing signs for complexes to names only. And in the 3.2's the remarks about analysis (3.24a–c, 3.25) and the remarks about definition (3.24d, 3.26) are mixed together in a way which gives the impression that they are not separate subjects. And this impression gets strong support from the *Notebooks*. On one occasion Wittgenstein writes:[1]

But suppose that we did not bother at all about the question of analysability? . . . Suppose then we were to say: The fact that a proposition is further analysable is shown in our further analysing it by means of definitions, and we work with it in every case exactly as if it were analysable.

Here Wittgenstein talks about analysis of propositions and analysis by definition, meaning the same thing by them. Then he writes in a later entry:[2]

But it is clear that components of our propositions can be analysed by means of a definition, and must be, if we want to approximate to the real structure of the proposition. *At any rate, then, there is a process of analysis.* And can it not now be asked whether this process comes to an end? And if so: what will the end be?

If it is true that every defined sign signifies *via* its definitions then presumably the chain of definitions must sometime have an end.

[1] *Nbk.* 11.10.14b.
[2] *Nbk.* 9.5.15c, d; italics Wittgenstein's; see also 13.5.15d. This view is most concisely expressed at *NM* 110.35–36: 'an *unanalysable* proposition = one in which only fundamental symbols = ones not capable of *definition*, occur'; italics Wittgenstein's.

And here the process of analysis that Wittgenstein talks about must be analysis in the chief sense, analysis as described in 2.0201. What he asks is whether this process comes to an end, and he appears to think it a possible answer that it will end because the chain of definitions must eventually have an end. Now, how on the usual interpretation of analysis can analysis and definition be thought of as the same process? Transferring descriptions from a subject to a predicate place does not define anything. Yet Wittgenstein seems to think analysis does.

These are the difficulties that I find with the usual interpretation. How should it be amended?

## 4. *Analysis* (2)

On the subject of analysis as understood in the *Tractatus*, I think we have a piece of exegesis by Wittgenstein himself. He writes in *Philosophical Investigations*:[1]

When I say: 'My broom is in the corner',—is this really a statement about the broomstick and the brush? Well, it could at any rate be replaced by a statement giving the position of the stick and the position of the brush. And this statement is surely a further analysed form of the first one.—But why do I call it 'further analysed'?—Well, if the broom is there, that surely means that the stick and brush must be there, and in a particular relation to one another; and this was as it were hidden in the sense of the first sentence, and is *expressed* in the analysed sentence.

Wittgenstein's example is: 'the broom is in the corner'. This was supposed to be analysed:

$$(\exists x)\,(Bx.Cx)$$

$Bx$: '$x$ is a broom'
$Cx$: '$x$ is in the corner'

But Wittgenstein analyses it into the following three propositions:

(i) the stick is in the corner.
(ii) the brush is in the corner.
(iii) the stick is attached to the brush.

Now, if this *is* the kind of analysis described in the *Tractatus*,

[1] *PI* para. 60.

then analysis consists not in shifting the description 'broom' from subject to predicate position but, roughly speaking, in breaking it up into sub-descriptions, which remain in the subject position. Presumably, since 'brush' and 'stick', which are now the subjects of our propositions, look as much like descriptions of complexes as 'broom' did, they too must undergo analysis. Presumably analysis will go on until we reach completely simple objects and names. Wittgenstein also says something in the *Investigations* about this repeated analysis:[1]

'A *name* signifies only what is an *element* of reality. What cannot be destroyed; what remains the same in all changes.'—But what is that? —Why, it swam before our minds as we said the sentence! This was the very expression of a quite particular image: of a particular picture which we want to use. For certainly experience does not show us these elements. We see *component parts* of something composite (of a chair, for instance). We say that the back is part of the chair, but is in turn itself composed of several bits of wood; while a leg is a simple component part. We also see a whole which changes (is destroyed) while its component parts remain unchanged. These are the materials from which we construct that picture of reality.

The general idea behind analysis, Wittgenstein says, is this. We see that a certain thing can be analysed into component things. For example:

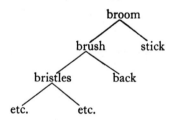

We also see that a thing can change while its components remain unaltered. We hypothesize that this must hold for every object there is: if it is subject to change, then it has parts into which it can be analysed which do not change. Eventually we reach components which cannot change. And, says Wittgenstein at the start of this passage, in this picture of the world these are the

---

[1] *PI* para. 59.

*elements* of reality and they can only be *named*. He says, in other words, that the analysis of the description 'broom' into 'brush' and 'stick' ends when names are reached.

One thing which straight away strengthens the idea that this is *Tractatus* analysis is that analysis is spoken of in these terms not only in the *Investigations* but in the *Notebooks* too. These *Investigations* passages could easily be entries from the *Notebooks*. We see what analysis means in the *Notebooks* in the course of a debate Wittgenstein carries on with himself over naming:[1]

What is my fundamental thought when I talk about simple objects? Do not 'complex objects' in the end satisfy just the demands which I apparently make on the simple ones? If I give this book a name . . .

Can I not give this book a name, in spite of its having parts? Do the parts matter, since what I want to name, though composed of them, is nevertheless still one single thing? From this we can see that a complex is something like a book. And simples are things like the basic elements of the book. And of basic elements Wittgenstein says quite a lot:[2]

As examples of the simple I always think of points of the visual field (just as parts of the visual field always come before my mind as typical composite objects).

And this way of thinking leads him to generalize:[3]

Is spatial complexity also logical complexity? It surely seems to be.

But to digress for just a moment: one should not make too much out of the sense-datum tendency in Wittgenstein's language in these entries, because he says exactly the same thing (namely, points are the simples and constitute complexes) in material object language. He says, in an entry I quoted before:[4]

The division of the body into *material points*, as we have it in physics, is nothing more than analysis into *simple components*.

And Wittgenstein alternates so easily and apparently unconsciously between sense-datum talk and material object talk that it

---

[1] *Nbk.* 14.6.15c.    [2] *Nbk.* 6.5.15d; see also 24.5.15b, c, 18.6.15e, 19.6.15a.
[3] *Nbk.* 7.5.15a; see also 7.5.15b *et seq.*, 17.6.15f.
[4] *Nbk.* 20.6.15m; see also 21.6.15f.

looks as if for him they amount to much the same thing. This is certainly the impression the *Notebooks* give, and, for what confirmation it lends, the *Tractatus* later says as much when it equates realism and idealism.[1] I shall be coming back to this topic later on.[2] Now, as for material objects Wittgenstein offers a variety of examples. Complex material objects are, in addition to books,[3] things like watches,[4] steamships and pencil strokes,[5] sentences, letters, and knives.[6] And in all of these cases the things are complex because they can be broken up into smaller material objects, just as spatial areas can be divided into sub-areas. Now, this gives an indication of what analysis is like. Analysis is the process of translating a statement about a complex into statements about its components,[7] and this process will go on until there is the same numerical multiplicity in our propositions as there is in the world,[8] and this will be until propositions make mention only of simples. This is exactly the analysis described in the *Investigations*. I said that the passages I quoted from the *Investigations* could well be entries in the *Notebooks*. Compare this *Investigations* passage:[9]

We see *component parts* of something composite (of a chair, for instance). We say that the back is part of the chair, but is in turn itself composed of several bits of wood . . .

with the *Notebooks* entry:[10]

A proposition like 'this chair is brown' seems to say something enormously complicated, for if we wanted to express this proposition in such a way that nobody could raise objections to it on grounds of ambiguity, it would have to be infinitely long.

Wittgenstein's reasons for saying this in the *Notebooks* are explained in what he says in the *Investigations*.

What, finally, is the most convincing evidence that this is *Tractatus* analysis is the way it fits the *Tractatus* itself.

(1) It fits the language of 2.0201. 2.0201 says that in analysis we reduce a statement about a complex to (i) a statement about its

---

[1] See 5.6's, esp. 5.64; cf. *Nbk.* 15.10.16u.       [2] See Ch. XI.3.
[3] *Nbk.* 23.5.15f, 14.6.15c.       [4] *Nbk.* 15.6.15c, 16.6.15a, h, k.
[5] *Nbk.* 25.4.15e.       [6] *Nbk.* 19.5.15a–c.       [7] See esp. *Nbk.* 17.6.15e–g.
[8] See esp. *Nbk.* 12.10.14a, 9.5.15c, e–g.
[9] *PI* para. 59.       [10] *Nbk.* 19.9.14.

constituents, and (ii) those propositions which describe the complex completely, that is, as the *Notes on Logic* add, that proposition which is equivalent to saying the complex exists. Now, the statement about the constituents of the complex is the compound statement: 'the stick and the brush are in the corner'. And the statement which completely describes the complex is the statement: 'the stick is attached to the brush'. That is, the complex broom is completely described by knowing that it is a stick attached to a brush. And this statement is equivalent to saying that the complex exists, because we know the complex exists if we know that these constituents are related in such a way as to constitute this complex entity.

(2) Then there is the close connexion between analysis and definition. Now the connexion is obvious. When I say 'the broom is in the corner', this is analysed into statements about the brush and the stick. In other words what I mean by the expression 'the broom' is now explained, i.e. defined, in the analysed form; by 'the broom' I mean 'the brush in a certain relation to the stick'.

(3) This solves another problem. In the *Tractatus* it looks as if Wittgenstein says that there are two kinds of elements in propositional signs proper: primitive signs and signs defined via primitive signs.[1] And it also looks as if primitive signs and names are the same thing; Wittgenstein does not say this, but for a number of reasons I think it is so. But, granting this, difficulties arise. Every element in a proposition will be either a name or defined by names. But this means that descriptive words like 'broom', 'brush' and 'stick' will be defined by names. But if names are of particulars, how can they define general words? 'Broom', after all, can be used to describe many things, and how can I possibly give the meaning of this general word in terms which refer to particular objects? It would almost seem on the basis of this that names, other evidence to the contrary, cannot be restricted to particulars. Now, however, we should see a way out of this difficulty. I said earlier that analysis explains that what I mean by 'the broom' is 'the brush in a certain relation to the stick'. What it explains, in other words, is what *I* mean *on this occasion*; I mean '*this* brush

[1] See esp. 3.261b.

in a certain relation to *this* stick'. And analysis is definition in this sense; by moving from statements about complexes to statements about particulars, I eventually define what I now mean by the signs in the unanalysed sentence.

(4) A consequence of this interpretation of analysis is that we are committed to saying that all names are names of particulars. The expression 'the broom' becomes 'the brush in a certain relation to the stick', and analysis will go on in this way until eventually we speak only of particulars and their relations. Where are any general terms now? Evidently all get analysed away. But note that on the fully analysed level instead of speaking of 'the broom' what we now speak of are 'these particulars in this configuration and these other particulars in that configuration, &c.' So, it looks as if configurations take over the role of general terms. As Wittgenstein tells us,[1] the configuration of names in a proposition says that the objects in reality are configured in a certain way. And, thus, since particulars configured in such and such a way constitute a broom, names configured in such and such a way will say that these objects constitute a broom. The role of general words in propositions is, in other words, taken over in the elementary proposition by the configurations of its signs. This, I think, we are also committed to saying. And for a number of reasons I think this is exactly what we should have to say. I want here to make three linguistic points that help show this, then I shall go on to some non-linguistic ones.

(i) An existent state of affairs is, by definition, a configuration of objects. And, as I just remarked, by configuring the names in an elementary proposition in a certain way, we say that the objects are configured in reality in such and such a way. This alone makes it difficult to take names as anything but names of particulars. If both '$\phi$' and '$a$' in the proposition '$\phi a$' were names, i.e. if subject-predicate propositions were elementary, then there would be objects corresponding to both the '$\phi$' and the '$a$'. But what sense does it make to say that these 'objects' are *configured* in the fact? It is certainly stretching things to say, for example, that red and a particular have a configuration in the fact that the particular is

[1] 2.15, 3.21.

red. (ii) Then the *Tractatus* seems to imply that by altering the configuration of the same objects we get new facts;[1] configuration, in other words, is accidental. But this could not be the case were $\phi$ as well as $a$ an object. Even allowing that in the fact that $\phi a$ there is a configuration of $\phi$ and $a$, it is hard to see what it would mean to say that they could have various configurations, that any one configuration is accidental. The only sense that I can see in saying that $\phi$ and $a$ are configured is to say the configuration is something on the order of $\phi$'s inhering in $a$, and this is not a configuration that could be changed. (iii) Then there is the matter of the naturalness of the language. In the *Tractatus* Wittgenstein speaks of elementary propositions as combinations of names, and of states of affairs as combinations of objects, with no special explanation of what he means by 'names' or 'objects'. But unless there was a radical change in the way he himself used these words, then by 'object' he must have meant particulars and so by 'names' names of particulars. For in *Notes on Logic* names were things like '$a$' in '$\phi a$' and '$a$' and '$b$' in '$aRb$'; '$\phi x$' and '$xRy$' were forms.[2] And in the *Notebooks*, in spite of the debate as to whether complexes are not in a way simple, in either case, simple or not, they are particulars, and their really simple components therefore will also be particulars.

(5) It looks on quite separate, non-linguistic evidence as though Wittgenstein would not accept propositions of the form '$\phi a$' as elementary. At 4.123 he says:

A property is internal if it is unthinkable that its object should not possess it.
(This shade of blue and that one stand, *eo ipso*, in the internal relation of lighter to darker. It is unthinkable that *these* two objects should not stand in this relation.)
(Here the shifting use of the word 'object' corresponds to the shifting use of the words 'property' and 'relation'.)

An internal property Wittgenstein defines as a property of structures.[3] Structure, he makes clear in this discussion[4] and it is also clear from the way the word is used throughout the

---

[1] See esp. 2.0271, 2.031, 3.1431.  [2] See esp. *NL* II 8.
[3] 4.122b.  [4] 4.122a.

*Tractatus*,[1] is something which facts have and which objects do not have. That is, objects in the strict sense. And this explains what the last paragraph in 4.123 must mean. If a shade of blue can have an internal property, then it also has a structure; and if it has a structure, then it cannot be an object in the strict sense. It is called an object because it and a darker blue are spoken of as standing in a relation to one another, and speaking loosely we can call terms of a relation objects. So, at least when the '$\phi$' in '$\phi a$' is a colour, '$\phi$' cannot refer to an object and '$\phi a$' cannot be elementary. Now, it looks as though Wittgenstein says: it cannot be elementary because anything blue has a structure to it which analysis would reveal. In other words, to say '*a* is blue' is to say objects *m, n, o,* . . . are configured in such and such a way. The '*a*' in '*a* is blue' must therefore be complex. A blue object is an object whose elements have a certain structure. Now, this way of talking, along with Wittgenstein's earlier talk of physicists' points as examples of simples, makes his account of blue very close to that of physics: a blue object is blue because its surface is structured in a certain way, and it is blue rather than, say, red, because to be red it would have to be structured differently. Once this idea occurs to us, if we then look back to the *Notebooks*, I think we find some corroboration:[2]

A point cannot be red and green at the same time: at first sight there seems no need for this to be a logical impossibility. But the very language of physics reduces it to a kinetic impossibility. We see that there is a difference of structure between red and green.

And then physics arranges them in a series. And then we see how here the true structure of the objects is brought to light.

And again:[3]

That the colours are not properties is shown by the analysis of physics, by the internal relations in which physics displays the colours.

So much for colours. But colours are only one kind of property. What of the rest? This last entry from the *Notebooks* has the short note attached:[4]

Apply this to sounds too.

[1] See esp. 2.032, 2.034, 2.15b, 5.13.          [2] *Nbk.* 16.8.16a, b.
[3] *Nbk.* 11.9.16b.          [4] *Nbk.* 11.9.16c.

Sounds, too, have internal structures. To say that '*a* is loud' is to say, as the physics of sound propagation shows, that the elements which constitute the sound *a* are structured in a particular way. All right, then, colours and sounds. But this still leaves other properties. Consider another *Notebooks* entry:[1]

Let us suppose we were to see a circular patch: is the circular form its *property*? Certainly not. It seems to be a structural 'property'. And if I notice that a spot is round, am I not noticing an infinitely complicated structural property?

So, circularity is not a property; it is a structural 'property'. And structural 'properties' are not properties in the strict sense because they can be analysed away. If I say 'this is circular', on analysis this becomes something like 'this object configured thusly with that, and that with that, . . .'. What we try to say by the property 'circular' is said by the configuration of the names in the elementary propositions, because this configuration says that the objects are configured in a certain way, which is what circularity is. So, both colours and shapes, i.e. what we see, and sounds, i.e. what we hear, turn out to be analysable. How much more does this leave? These are, at any rate, good grounds for entertaining seriously the idea that Wittgenstein thinks all '$\phi$''s in '$\phi a$' are to be analysed away. All facts, it seems, are quite literally objects in some configuration.

(6) This enables us to explain 4.23. Names, 4.23 says, occur in propositions only in the nexus of an elementary proposition. This too is to be taken literally. When we analyse a statement about a complex, names appear when and only when we reach the last stage of the analysis. In analysing 'the broom is in the corner' we pass through several stages in which we talk of the brush and the stick and then, presumably, of sub-descriptions of these. The final stage comes when, leaving descriptions altogether, we mention only particulars. Thus, names appear only in the final stage.

(7) This means that a name will appear in a proposition only when all the rest of the signs in it are names too. This, in turn, would seem to mean that since the propositional sign '$\phi a$' has the sign '$\phi$' in it, which is not a name, '*a*' cannot be a name. I

---

[1] *Nbk.* 18.6.15j.

think there is evidence that Wittgenstein believes this. Consider 3.221. 'Objects can only be named'; in other words, I cannot describe them; I cannot say of an object that it is a $\phi$. 3.221 does not say just this, but I think we can surmise it. It does say that I can only state *how* a thing is and not *what* it is. That I can only say *how* a thing is means, I think, that I can only say how an object stands in relation to other objects; I can only give its configuration with other objects. This is purely external information, and to say of an object, for example, that it is blue would have to be counted as internal information, information about the object itself and not merely about its configurations. It would be internal, because a statement like '*a* is blue', if *a* is an object, could not be accidental. All change, Wittgenstein tells us,[1] comes from alteration in the configurations of objects. But *a*, being simple, has no internal configuration to alter, so it could not possibly change from blue to some other colour. If an object, a simple, answers to a certain description, then it must always answer to it. The only way to avoid this conclusion is to say that $\phi$ and *a* themselves are what is configured. So, to the extent that saying that $\phi$ and *a* have a configuration makes one uncomfortable, one should be willing to accept that '$\phi a$' is not elementary.

(8) This now enables us to explain a previously puzzling feature of *Notes on Logic*, viz. Wittgenstein's division of propositional elements into two kinds, names ('*a*', '*b*', &c.) and forms ('$\phi x$', '$xRy$', &c.). And this way of talking continues on into the *Notebooks*:[2]

. . . we don't have any examples before our minds when we use Fx and all the other variable form-signs.

Why forms? Now we can see that, once again, he means this literally. Propositional elements like '$\phi x$' and '$xRy$' have to do with the form only of the fact they depict. And in analysis we do away with all signs which have to do with the form of the fact so that in the end the contents of our proposition correspond to the contents of the fact and the form (configuration) of these propositional elements expresses what the form (configuration) of the fact is. The

---

[1] 2.0271.          [2] *Nbk.* 19.6.15c.

'$\phi$' in '$\phi x$', having nothing to do with the content of the fact, cannot have an object corresponding to it and thus cannot be a name. Nor, consequently, can '$\phi a$' be elementary.

(9) Then there is the important, though not entirely clear, testimony of 4.24, where Wittgenstein explains his symbolism. Names are indicated by single letters, such as '$x$', '$y$', '$z$'; elementary propositions are written as functions of names, like '$fx$', '$\phi(x, y)$'. So, by explicit admission, the '$\phi$' in '$\phi a$' is not a name. But before I can claim the support of 4.24 I must tend to some of the problems which, as I pointed out in Chapter II.4, it poses. If, as 4.24 says, '$\phi$' is not a name, and since, as we know, elementary propositions contain only names,[1] then how can '$\phi a$' be elementary, which 4.24 also says? And if '$\phi$' is not a name, the proposition '$\phi a$' contains only one name and its fact one object;[2] so 4.24 conflicts with 4.22, which defines an elementary proposition as a connexion of names (plural), and with 2.0272, which defines a state of affairs as a configuration of objects (plural). It is this impasse, I suppose, that has led many people to say that '$\phi$' must, after all, be a name. But besides the awkwardness of making '$\phi$' a name, there is Wittgenstein's unambiguous assertion that '$\phi x$' is not a name but a function of names. Nor is the impasse avoided any more successfully by allowing that '$\phi a$' contains only one name and its fact one object, but by claiming that it is the limiting case for combination of names and objects for there to be only one name or one object. This explanation simply fails to account for the fact that the '$\phi$' in '$\phi a$' plays an important part in characterizing the sense of the proposition. '$\phi$' says something and cannot be ignored. Also, all propositional elements are either primitive signs or defined by primitive signs. But '$\phi$' cannot be primitive, unless we want to claim that more than names are primitive. Nor can it be defined, because this would mean that it could be resolved into the names which defined it, in which case '$\phi a$' would not be elementary. What we must say about 4.24, I think, is this. The present account of analysis shows that objects are always particulars, that names can only be names of particulars, and that subject-predicate propositions cannot be elementary.

---

[1] 3.2–3.202.  [2] 2.131, 3.203, 3.22.

All of this agrees fully with 4.24, except for Wittgenstein's saying that an elementary proposition can be written as a function of names, e.g. '$\phi x$'. But I think there is a straightforward way of accommodating this statement too. Suppose, as the *Tractatus* says in several places, that an elementary proposition is a combination of names and that names are things like '$a$', '$b$', '$c$', '$d$', &c. Now, suppose the objects named by the four signs I have just given are of such a form that the minimum combination possible is of four elements; then we could write the elementary proposition:

$$\text{'}a\text{-}b\text{-}c\text{-}d\text{'}$$

where this configuration of the signs expresses something about the configuration of the four objects. Now, as Wittgenstein says both at 4.24 and elsewhere,[1] this proposition is a function of the expressions contained in it. To show what expressions are contained in it I change one or more of its elements into variables, leaving the rest constant.[2] Suppose I substitute a variable for '$a$':

$$\text{'}x\text{-}b\text{-}c\text{-}d\text{'}$$

According to Wittgenstein, this is one of the expressions the proposition contains. I can, for convenience, use a compact sign to mark it, say '$\phi x$'. So, when I substitute '$a$' back again, I have '$\phi a$'. Now, this proposition is a function of '$a$', a function, that is, of whatever sign we substitute in the variable place. This is what I take Wittgenstein to mean when he says that an elementary proposition can be written as a function of names.

I should add that this view is also adopted by G. E. M. Anscombe,[3] though she adopts it because it is the best way of making sense of 4.24 and some closely related propositions (I agree in this), and not because she shares any of the views about analysis I have been propounding. But there is also something important in what she says that I disagree with. She speaks of the '$\phi$' in '$\phi a$' as a cover for names.[4] I have just given a sense in which I think this is true; elementary propositions can be expressed in the form '$\phi a$', where '$\phi$' is a cover for names. But this is true only for

---

[1] 3.318.          [2] See 3.312, 3.313.
[3] G. E. M. Anscombe: op. cit., pp. 98–102.          [4] Ibid., p. 99.

elementary propositions. This is an important proviso. Miss Anscombe goes on to treat functions generally in this way,[1] for example, the function 'red' in the proposition '*a* is red'. 'Red', being a function, covers names; let us say, quite arbitrarily, three names: ' –*b*–*c*–*d*'. Thus, we can translate the proposition into the familiar form:

$$`a\text{-}b\text{-}c\text{-}d`$$

But I think we cannot. And Wittgenstein's example of analysis from the *Investigations*, I have been arguing, shows this. Whenever I say '*a* is a broom' the *a* must be complex, because what the proposition says is that *a*'s elements are configured in a certain way. Thus, the analysis is not '*a* is –*b*–*c*–*d*' but rather '*e*–*f*–*g*–*h*', where these are names for the constituents of the complex named by '*a*'. This is important because unless one makes this distinction, it would look as if the *Tractatus* view that elementary propositions are always relational does not amount to much. The only difference between a proposition of the form '$\phi a$' and one of the form '*a*–*b*–*c*' would be that '$\phi$' covers names, and '$\phi a$' could as well have been expressed in the form '*a*–*b*–*c*' (or something like it). But in most cases, in the case of true, i.e. *general*, predicates and not of functions which are short-hand for names of particulars, the analysis is quite different. The '$\phi$' is, as Wittgenstein said in the *Notes*, a form; it has to do with the configuration of the fact and not with any of its ultimate constituents.

(10) I conclude the evidence *pro* this account of analysis with a number of small but interesting items, which I group together here.

(i) During one of the periods in the *Notebooks* when he was tempted by the idea that complexes, too, were simple, Wittgenstein wrote:[2]

What seems to be given us *a priori* is the concept: *This.*—Identical with the concept of the *object*.

In other words, when I speak of objects, what I mean is the kind of thing that I can indicate by gesturing and uttering 'this'. And the point, as it appears from the context, is that this condition seems to

---

[1] Ibid., pp. 109–11.    [2] *Nbk.* 16.6.15d.

hold as much for complexes as for simples. Then the very next entry is:[1]

Relations and properties, &c. are *objects* too.

From the context this seems definitely to be saying: since the concept *object* and the concept *this* are the same, and since we have the feeling of *this* with complexes, then even relations and properties can be counted as objects. And this is good evidence that otherwise Wittgenstein would not count them as objects and that in the strict sense they certainly are not objects.

(ii) Propositions put out feelers, so to speak, running from the elements of the picture, the names, to the elements of what is pictured, the objects. This is how the picture touches reality.[2] The metaphor suggests that objects must be particulars. When I picture a fact, I picture a particular fact, a particular part of reality. And it would seem that any connexions I draw from the picture to the fact would have to be to particulars. This claim is supported by Wittgenstein's one illustration of the metaphor, which comes in the *Notebooks*:[3]

Do I really draw a feeler in when I say ( $\exists x$). $\phi x$ instead of $\phi a$?

Here the feeler runs to a particular.

(iii) There is the obviously important remark at 2.0251:[4]

Space, time, and colour (being coloured) are forms of objects.

This is a difficult remark, but one can make some plausible guesses about it. The form of an object, we know, is its possibilities of combination with other objects. Now, assuming my interpretation of 4.123 to be right, anything which is coloured is composed of objects in certain configurations. Perhaps it would make sense, therefore, to say that these objects have a certain form which other objects do not. The same explanation appears to work for space and time. From my account of analysis it follows that there are objects which in combination constitute the three-dimensional spatial entities which populate the world. And it would seem that the same considerations which led Wittgenstein to analyse statements about complexes, where the complexes are spatial, into simples,

---

[1] *Nbk.* 16.6.15e.    [2] 2.1515.    [3] *Nbk.* 15.10.14g.
[4] See also 2.171b; also 2.0121d, 2.0131a.

would make him do it for temporal complexes as well. When I speak of, say, the past hour, as in a statement like 'he has been speaking for the past hour', does this not mean that he has been speaking for the past minute and the minute before and so on? So there are objects of time as well, which in combination constitute the temporal complexes of which we speak. And they would have a different form, it would seem, from spatial objects. At first sight the idea of temporal objects probably strikes one as odd, but there is something in the *Notebooks* which warrants giving the idea serious consideration. After several weeks in which Wittgenstein had been thinking about the analysis of material bodies down to simples there comes an entry which goes, *in toto*:[1]

Spatial and *temporal* complexes.

This apparently is Wittgenstein reminding himself: there are, after all, other kinds of complexes than material bodies; there are temporal complexes, and on analysis they will reduce to simple components and thus to objects of a different kind from spatial simples. Now, if these guesses are right, or near right, then spatial, temporal, and colour objects are three examples of objects. And though we by no means have reason to think that these are all possible examples, still, as far as they go, they support my thesis. Objects are particulars, and analysis is analysis of statements about complexes composed of these kinds of objects into statements about these objects alone and their configuration.

## 5. *An Alternative Theory of Descriptions*

All the same—it might be objected at about this point—there is also strong evidence favouring the Russellian view, and though you may be able to give evidence against it and evidence for another view, it is quite possible that the *Tractatus* does not speak clearly enough for this issue to be settled. I think that the evidence an objector would have foremost in mind is 3.24, which goes in part:

When a propositional element signifies a complex, this can be seen from an indeterminateness in the propositions in which it occurs. In such cases we *know* that the proposition leaves something undetermined. (In fact the generality-sign *contains* a proto-picture.)

[1] *Nbk.* 22.5.15c; italics Wittgenstein's.

A proto-picture is what we get by changing any of the constants in a proposition to a variable: for example, from '$\phi a$' we can get the proto-picture '$\phi x$'.[1] Then, how the notation for generality contains a proto-picture is plain; a general, i.e. quantified, proposition is nothing but a proto-picture with the variable bound: for example, '$(\exists x)\ \phi x$'. What ought to occur to us right away is Russell's Theory of Descriptions. Propositions about complexes contain proto-pictures; in fact, they are disguised general statements. 'The book on the table is red' is to be translated:

$$( \exists x)\ (Bx.Tx.Rx)$$

And is this not good reason to think that Wittgenstein's analysis is modelled on Russell's? Statements about complexes, we could say, contain generality in the form of proto-pictures, and analysis is the translation by which this (real) form becomes manifest. I do not think this is enough, though, to change our minds. First, it still does not answer any of the arguments I set out against the Russellian interpretation. Second, I think we must be careful, no matter how natural the move looks, about taking even these references to generality and proto-pictures in the Russellian way. From the *Notebooks* it would seem that Wittgenstein had his own related but none the less different way of taking them, in short, his own related yet different theory of descriptions. Complexes can be given in propositions only by descriptions; this is said in both the *Notebooks* and the *Tractatus*.[2] Describing stands in contrast to naming; I cannot name a complex; it can only be described. How does a description present a complex in the proposition? To this, as we see from the *Notebooks*, Wittgenstein had a well thought out answer:[3]

... if I am talking about, e.g., this watch, and mean something complex by that and nothing depends upon the complexity, then a generalization will make its appearance in the proposition and the fundamental forms of the generalization will be completely determinate *so far as they are given at all.*

When I talk about a complex and thus give it a description, a generalization makes its appearance. A description, we can surmise,

[1] 3.315.        [2] 3.24b and *Nbk*. 15.5.15b.        [3] *Nbk*. 18.6.15c.

is of the form 'the $\phi$', because the description could always as well be predicated of the thing (e.g. '$(\exists x)\ \phi x$') as used as a description. And we know that the '$\phi$' in '$\phi a$' or in '$(\exists x)\ \phi x$' is a form; that is, it tells us about the structure of the fact it pictures and not the content. This is why descriptions are generalizations; they are empty of content. And this is why in this entry Wittgenstein speaks of 'the fundamental forms of the generalization'. That this is what he means becomes clear in other entries. He says:[1]

. . . the proposition describes the complex by means of its logical properties.

Describing a complex is giving the form of the objects which constitute it. So, when we say 'the broom is in the corner', this is to say 'the objects (unspecified) structured broomly are in the corner'. The advantage of descriptions comes, of course, from their making language simpler. Instead of having to refer individually to all the objects involved in a complex we simply refer to their form. It is, Wittgenstein remarks:[2]

. . . through generality that ordinary propositions get their stamp of simplicity.

And then, he says as well:[3]

Even if the sentences which we ordinarily use all contain generalizations, still there must surely occur in them the proto-pictures of the component parts of their special cases.

The sentences which we ordinarily use, sentences which employ descriptions, have occurring in them the proto-pictures of the component parts of the complexes they describe. The proto-pictures occur in the descriptions in these propositions in much the same way that, as Wittgenstein tells us,[4] proto-pictures occur in elementary propositions. The elementary proposition:

'$a$-$b$-$c$'

contains a proto-picture in that it can be looked at as the filling-out of this:

'$x$-$y$-$z$'

or, if we prefer, this:

'$(\ )$-$(\ )$-$(\ )$'

[1] *Nbk.* 20.10.14g.    [2] *Nbk.* 26.4.15a.    [3] *Nbk.* 7.5.15c.    [4] *Nbk.* 12.11.14e.

A proto-picture is a form not yet given content, and since this is what a description is, a description is a proto-picture. Now, this brings us to 'indeterminateness of sense'. Every picture is *a* complete picture, as both the *Tractatus* and *Notebooks* say,[1] only the *Notebooks* say it with some of the details:[2]

> If generalizations occur [in a proposition], then the forms of the particular cases must be manifest—and it is clear that this demand is justified, otherwise the proposition cannot be a picture at all, of *anything*.
> For if possibilities *are left open* in the proposition, *just this* must be determined: *what* is left open. The generalizations of the form—e.g.—must be determined. What I do not know I do not know, but the proposition must show me WHAT I know.

Generalizations come into consideration here because this is the obvious way in which a proposition can be less than completely informative; we leave out some of the content and speak instead of forms. Here Wittgenstein is saying that even though we do this and so in a way make our picture of the world incomplete, the picture is still a complete picture. It does not tell us everything, but, first, what it tells us it tells us in determinate terms and, second, it shows us what it leaves open, what is still indeterminate. But notice that the other side of the determinateness is an indeterminateness; in general, any proposition involving forms without full specification of the contents, e.g. involving descriptions, will be indeterminate in sense. Or, as we could put it (this is 3.24c again):

> When a propositional element signifies a complex, this can be seen from an indeterminateness in the propositions in which it occurs. In such cases we *know* that the proposition leaves something undetermined.

This interpretation of determinateness and indeterminateness of sense is borne out and elaborated by this entry in the *Notebooks*:[3]

> ... even when we want to express a *completely determinate* sense there is the possibility of failure. So it seems that we have, so to speak, no guarantee that our proposition is really a picture of reality.

---

[1] 5.156d; *Nbk.* 16.6.15m, see also j, l.
[2] *Nbk.* 17.6.15n, o.     [3] *Nbk.* 20.6.15 l–n, u.

The division of the body into *material points*, as we have it in physics, is nothing more than analysis into *simple components*.

But could it be possible that the sentences in ordinary use have, as it were, only an incomplete sense (quite apart from their truth or falsehood), and that the propositions in physics, as it were, approach the stage where a proposition really has a complete sense?

. . . are the propositions of physics and the propositions of ordinary life at bottom equally sharp, and does the difference consist only in the more consistent application of signs in the language of science?

Wittgenstein's answer was that propositions can have a perfectly determinate sense; the possibility of names is the possibility of determinateness of sense.[1] And this has brought us to analysis. We make our sense perfectly determinate by filling in the content-less forms, by translating our propositions into a version where we, like physicists, speak only of simples. And this reduction suggests the *Investigations* kind of analysis, a process by which the sense of a proposition is made more and more definite, until finally it is completely determinate and the analysis finished. I think that 3.24 can be accommodated to my interpretation of analysis; it might even be counted in its favour.

## 6. *Objects Are Simple*

I return now to the thesis of the 2.02's, of which the discussion of analysis is just one stage: objects are simple. Wittgenstein's proof is as follows. Objects form the substance of the world, therefore they cannot be compound, i.e. they must be simple.[2] And the world must have substance because: (i) if the world had no substance, then whether a proposition had sense would depend upon whether another proposition were true,[3] and (ii) if whether a proposition had sense depended upon another proposition's being true, then we could not sketch out a picture of the world, true or false.[4] The argument moves from the obvious falsity of the consequent in (ii): of course, we can make pictures of the world. The argument is in form a two-staged *modus tollens*; (i))$p \supset q$, (ii) $q \supset r$, but $\sim r$, thus $\sim q$, thus $\sim p$. And its conclusion, $\sim p$, is: the world does have substance, i.e. objects which are simple.

[1] 3.23.    [2] 2.021.    [3] 2.0211.    [4] 2.0212.

Because of the way the argument moves, I shall start with (ii). Without simple objects we should have no names, and without names language would be limited, in effect, to descriptions. Now, a proposition containing descriptions has an indeterminateness in its sense. That is, such a proposition can say various things about the world. We could try to remedy this by using more specific descriptions. Instead of talking about 'the broom' we could say 'the brush attached to the stick'. But we can never get rid of the indeterminateness entirely as long as we use descriptions at all. Thus, either eventually we reach names, and so can say with full determinateness what we claim about the world, or there is no end to the descriptions, in which case there will always be indeterminateness of sense. And while there is indeterminateness of sense, we shall never be able to picture a particular state of affairs, that is, to say that *it* exists; instead, we shall be limited to giving the form of several states of affairs, that is, to specifying a *class* of states of affairs. In the absence of simple objects and names, generality is never to be avoided and what precisely we mean never to be expressed.

This, I think, is the context within which this proof is to be understood. Without substance we could only make proto-pictures, never true pictures. This shows why for one proposition to have sense another proposition must be true. It shows us fairly clearly, first of all, what Wittgenstein means by the *sense* of a proposition. He means the particular picture the proposition presents on a single occasion of its use. When I utter a sentence, quantified ones aside, I claim to be picturing a particular piece of the world. On a different occasion I may with the same descriptions picture a different piece of the world, and in this case the sense will be different. For example, when I say 'the watch is on the table', meaning my watch and my table, and another persons says 'the watch is on the table', meaning his watch and his table, then what we picture is different. And since analysis reduces our propositions to names only, and since analysis is the method of making our *sense* more and more determinate, then both the analysis and the sense of our two propositions must be different. Now, taking *sense* in this way, Wittgenstein's argument is to be understood as follows. The expression 'the broom' in 'the broom is in the corner' needs further specification. I can specify what I mean by 'the broom' by using more specific descriptions. This is what I do in analysis; my propositions become: '(i) the brush is attached to the stick, (ii) the stick is in the corner, and (iii) the brush is in the corner'. The first proposition in the analysis specifies what I mean by 'the broom'. In order for me to be talking about anything at all, this proposition must be true. In other words, in general, the proposition that must be true in order for another to have sense is the proposition which, by specifying the application of the description, gives it a sense. But now we get into a regress, because the same indeterminateness holds for the descriptions I used in the proposition which gives the sense of the first description. What do I refer to in the world when I here speak of 'the brush' and 'the stick'? Unless we eventually reach names, the regress is infinite. The sense of a proposition will never be specified.

What I have just said is close to, yet not quite the same as saying that for the proposition to have sense what must be true is the existential proposition '$(\exists x)$ ($x$ is a broom)'. I have put it in this more complicated way, because I think what Wittgenstein says cannot be quite so simple. The existential proposition is not enough to get the argument going. It seems clear that Wittgenstein's argument involves an infinite regress. If in order for '$p$' to have sense '$q$' had to be true, then for '$q$' to have sense '$r$' would have to be true, and so on. And this is why we should never be able to form a picture of the world. But does the proposition '$(\exists x)$ ($x$ is a broom)' also require that another proposition be true? So far as I can tell, no further existential propositions at least are needed, because this proposition contains only one description and it has already been said that something answers to it. I remark about this, because there is the temptation to state or to abbreviate Wittgenstein's argument like this. But if we do, we should remember that strictly speaking this cannot be right and that Wittgenstein had in mind something closer to this more complicated account.

The rest of the 2.02's work out the consequences of this proof of substance. 2.027 sums them up; objects, the unalterable, and the subsistent are one and the same. Objects are the same as the unalterable, because what alteration there is comes as alteration in configuration.[1] This includes both variation between this and any imagined world and change which comes with the passage of time. It is hard to appreciate from the start just how extreme these two claims are, but the further one penetrates in the *Tractatus* the more one will be impressed by it. As to the first, there is an interesting commentary in the *Blue Book*. Wittgenstein talks at one point about the old problem of how we can think what is false, in particular about the feeling that when we think what is false the object of our thought must, paradoxically, be a non-existent fact. And on this he comments:[2]

We are here misled by the substantives 'object of thought' and 'fact', and by the different meanings of the word 'exist'.

Talking of the fact as a 'complex of objects' springs from this confusion (cf. *Tractatus Logico-philosophicus*). Supposing we asked: 'How can one *imagine* what does not exist?' The answer seems to be: 'If we do, we imagine non-existent combinations of existing elements'. A centaur doesn't exist, but a man's head and torso and arms and a horse's legs do exist. 'But can't we imagine an object utterly different from any one which exists?'—We should be inclined to answer: 'No; the elements, individuals, must exist . . .'.

The context this supplies to the remarks on imagining is helpful. There must exist certain things in order for there to be meaning, because I must say of at least some symbols simply that *this* means *that*. But we avoid the paradoxes of judging falsely when we realize that none of the symbols in this class is a proposition. Propositions, even elementary ones, are complexes of names, and, likewise, states of affairs are always complexes of objects. It is the objects which must exist for there to be meaning. So objects are the actual, and states of affairs the possible. One of the consequences of making states of affairs 'complexes of objects' is that it imposes a limit on imaginable worlds. If there are simples at the base of all facts, and we merely name them, and these names are, either in themselves or through the signs defined by them, the content of all our propositions, then any world that we can imagine will be imagined in terms of these names and so populated by these

[1] 2.0271.          [2] *Bl. Bk.* p. 31.

objects. Wittgenstein's position here is as extreme as it sounds: all that we can do in imagination is rearrange already existing elements. But I think we can make Wittgenstein admit one reservation. There is nothing to prevent us from imagining an impoverished world, a world which has different objects from this one by having fewer. We could, for example, imagine a non-spatial world. So far as I can see, there is no reason why Wittgenstein would not accept this. His requirement is merely that, whatever the content of our imagination, the only way for it to differ from things as they are is in the configuration the objects take on.

I have said that objects are fixed also in the sense of enduring through time. Wittgenstein never says this in so many words; yet he does seem to believe it. It would be hard for him not to, because enduring in imagination and enduring through time are not easily separated. Certainly one way I can imagine the world as different is by imagining changes of the kind that come with time. If not all, certainly most of the changes that come with time are imaginable, and thus in these changes the objects will remain constant. Then, also, part of what Wittgenstein says in the *Investigations* about analysis is that:[1]

'A *name* signifies only what is an *element* of reality. What cannot be destroyed; what remains the same in all changes.' . . . We say that the back is part of the chair, but is in turn itself composed of several bits of wood; while a leg is a simple component part. We also see a whole which changes (is destroyed) while its component parts remain unchanged. These are the materials from which we construct that picture of reality.

And if I am right about analysis, then this should be close to the *Tractatus* picture of reality. (The Excalibur example[2] in the *Investigations* will, if I am right, be relevant here too. It makes the same point: there must be simples which cannot be destroyed, because there must be names to which the fate of the name 'Excalibur' cannot occur). Then there is the language of 2.0271:

Objects are what is unalterable and subsistent; their configuration is what is changing and unstable.

Neither 2.0271 nor any of the surrounding propositions puts any

[1] *PI* para. 59.    [2] *PI* para. 39; see also paras. 41, 50, 55; see also Ch. XI.4.

qualifications on the sense of 'change', which makes the whole proposition sound as if it says that objects do not change with time, this being the sense of change which would first come to mind.

For these reasons I think Wittgenstein does believe objects endure temporally too. Whether he has given himself good grounds for this is a different matter. I think probably not. The proof that there is substance and his hypothesis that all propositional elements are either names or defined by names are sufficient only for the imagination half of his thesis. Objects endure in imagination because *at any given time* there are only certain elements out of which the pictures of our imaginings can be constructed. But this does not mean that with time both the objects and thus the names could not be different. So this, at any rate, is not enough for the time half of the thesis, and I can see nothing now to make up the deficiency. But if there is not quite a proof for the time thesis, there are considerations which make it look plausible and which may well explain why Wittgenstein was led to adopt it. One of the consequences of what Wittgenstein says about substance is:[1]

Substance is what subsists independently of what is the case.

What more can change in time be than change in what is the case? If nothing more, then objects endure through time. So, accept this identity and the time thesis follows. And I think that in the *Tractatus* Wittgenstein must have accepted both it and its consequence.

## 7. *Aristotelian and* Tractatus *Substance*

I can sum up the 2.02's with Wittgenstein's own striking phrase:[2]

In a manner of speaking, objects are colourless.

Or in more detail:[3]

The substance of the world *can* only determine a form, and not any material properties. For it is only by means of propositions that material properties are represented—only by the configuration of objects that they are produced.

[1] 2.024.  [2] 2.0232.  [3] 2.0231.

Material properties ('materielle Eigenschaften') are contrasted with internal properties; that is, they are the same as the 'externe Eigenschaften' Wittgenstein goes on to speak of in 2.0233. And Wittgenstein says that objects by themselves determine no material, no real properties; real properties are first constituted by objects entering into configurations. Thus, whenever we attribute some real property '$\phi$' to an entity, this is to say that there are objects configured in a certain way, because it is only with the appearance of objects in configuration that such properties appear.

This makes clear, I think, how misleading one of the interpretive commonplaces about the *Tractatus* is: that Wittgenstein's *substance* is the same as Aristotle's *first substance*.[1] This identity has been used many a time as ground for the judgement that the *Tractatus* leads to a metaphysical morass. Perhaps Aristotelian first substance is a metaphysical morass, and perhaps the *Tractatus* does lead to one; but if so, these facts are independent. An Aristotelian first substance, true enough, has no real properties, but it is that which can have real properties affirmed of it. It has neither shape, nor colour, &c., because it is that to which we attribute shape, colour, &c. But Wittgensteinian substance has neither shape nor colour, simply because these, and all other real properties, have to do with the configurations of objects. It is only complexes of objects that can have real properties, because to attribute a real property to an entity is to say that this entity has a certain configuration, and this, of course, is not the sort of thing that can be said of one object.

In sum, objects are colourless. Or to put this literally: where real properties are concerned, objects are propertyless—property-less not in the sense that they are what *bear* the properties, but in the sense that they are what *make* the properties.

[1] See, e.g., J. O. Urmson: *Philosophical Analysis*, pp. 57 ff.; J. R. Searle: 'Proper Names', p. 169.

# VII

## STATES OF AFFAIRS

### 1. *Introductory*

IN the second two of the four parts of the 2.0's Wittgenstein takes up states of affairs; in the 2.03's he considers how they are formed by the combination of objects, and in 2.04, 2.05, and the 2.06's he considers their existence and non-existence. For now I want to discuss only two matters concerning states of affairs: the distinction Wittgenstein draws between their *form* and *structure*, and his puzzling claim that the existence or non-existence of one of them does not affect the existence or non-existence of any other.

### 2. *Their Form and Structure*

One of the much cited aphorisms of the *Tractatus* is that a proposition is a fact.[1] What this means is that a proposition is not just a set, a jumble, of names;[2] the names must have a configuration;[3] and the fact which is a proposition is that *these* names stand in *this* configuration. In the 2.03's Wittgenstein makes an analogous point. In a state of affairs objects are related in a *determinate* way.[4] A state of affairs is not just a jumble of objects; they have *a* combination; vary the particular combination and you vary the state of affairs.

What is most important in the 2.03's is that this definite combination of objects has, Wittgenstein says, both *structure* and *form*. And it is hard to see what he wants this distinction to mark. All he says in definition of the two terms is this:[5]

The determinate way in which objects are connected in a state of affairs is the structure of the state of affairs.
Its form is the possibility of its structure.

Now, this makes it seem as if structure is simply configuration, and as if, therefore, states of affairs with different objects can have their structure (configuration) in common. This is what in the

---

[1] 2.141, 3.14b.　　[2] 3.141–2.　　[3] 3.1431b; see also 4.0311.
[4] 2.031.　　[5] 2.032–3.

end I want to say, but the two persons who, to my knowledge, have paid most attention to the matter have decided that this cannot be so. F. P. Ramsey, in his review of the *Tractatus*, admits that this is how things look, but thinks that, none the less, certain remarks Wittgenstein makes later in the *Tractatus* mean that structure involves objects as well as configurations, and that, consequently, 'two different facts never have the same structure'.[1] And B. F. McGuinness thinks that the later remarks which show this are 4.1211, 5.13, 5.2, and 5.22.[2] The argument goes: Wittgenstein says that we can recognize from their structures when one proposition follows from another (5.13), or, generally, when one proposition stands in any logical relation to another (5.2, 5.22). Take contradiction, which is one of the logical relations we recognize from structure (4.1211). To recognize that two propositions are contradictory we must know that they are, say, '*aRb*' and '$\sim aRb$'; it does not do to know that they are '( )R( )' and '$\sim$( )R( )', because were this enough '*p*' could be the contradictory of '$\sim q$'. The structure of propositions, therefore, must involve names, and the structure of states of affairs objects. And this means that a structure is equivalent to a state of affairs and vice versa; there is no difference between asserting the existence of a structure and asserting the existence of a state of affairs. As for form, saying that form is the possibility of structure will mean this. The structure *aRb*, i.e. the state of affairs *aRb*, is of all of the following forms (arranged in ascending order of generality): '*xRy*', '$\phi(x, y)$', '*this is how things stand*'. Any one of these forms is the possibility of this structure in that this structure is a possible way of filling out these forms.

I am disposed, as I have said, to take structure much more in accord with our first impressions of 2.032. I do not see why these later remarks of Wittgenstein's should change our mind. Certainly we need more information than '( )R( )' and '$\sim$( )R( )' to know that two propositions are contradictory. But we do not need to know what names fill these brackets. All we must know is, given

---

[1] F. P. Ramsey: *The Foundations of Mathematics*, pp. 271–2.
[2] B. F. McGuinness: 'Pictures and Form in Wittgenstein's *Tractatus*', pp. 214–16, see esp. n. 13.

any set of names, how they would be distributed in the brackets. What we must know, in other words, is given by the propositional variables '$xRy$' and '$\sim xRy$'. So, for all that Wittgenstein says in these later passages, structure need not involve names. If anything, I should think it more likely that these passages indicate that structure does not involve names, that in these passages Wittgenstein is making the usual point that inference, contradiction, &c., do not depend on the material content of the propositions. Now, as regards form, I think this interpretation meets quite separate difficulties in connexion with the picture theory. A picture and the fact it pictures must have a certain form in common, and it is in virtue of this shared form that the first can be a picture of the second.[1] The form they must have in common is pictorial form ('Form der Abbildung'), also called logical form ('logische Form').[2] Now, as interpreted above, we determine the form of the structure $aRb$ by successively removing its constant elements. Suppose the state of affairs consists of the two objects, $a$ and $b$, an inch away from one another, like this:

$$a\text{————————}b$$

Supposedly, we can represent one of its forms in this way:

Now, one way we could picture this state of affairs existing would be to place two elements an inch away from one another. That is, we can use a picture which itself is a fact of the form represented above. But, of course, the picture need not share this particular form; pictures can be less identical with the facts than this and still be their pictures. So, the form represented above (if indeed it is a form) is not pictorial form, not logical form. Consider, then, the next more general form; we get this by no longer holding the relation 'one inch from one another' constant; what results is a form which we can express as 'two objects in some relation to one another', or, more briefly, as '$\phi(x, y)$'. But if this is pictorial form, logical form (and it is certainly general enough; we need not go further), then the picture theory begins to look rather weak.

[1] 2.16, 2.161.          [2] 2.17, 2.18.

Wittgenstein's claim that picture and fact must have pictorial form in common would be nothing more than the claim, which he also makes in another place,[1] that picture and fact must have the same numerical multiplicity. All facts, anyway, are objects in some determinate relation to one another, so all that we need demand of one fact for it to picture another is that it contain the same number of objects. I think, however, that the picture theory has more point to it than this, and that the demand for identity in logical form is not just a demand for the same numerical multiplicity. I shall try to prove this in the next chapter, where I go into the picture theory in detail.

I say that structure is the configuration of the objects in the state of affairs. And as configuration is sharable, so structure is sharable. To illustrate, suppose we have six spatial objects, *a* to *f*, all with the same form, i.e. capable of entering the same (spatial) configurations. Then the two states of affairs

have, on my account, the same structure. Consider the first of the two more closely. We would say that what makes its configuration possible is that each of its elements is of such a form that it can combine with the other elements. So, what makes this particular structure (configuration) possible also makes other configurations of these same elements possible. In other words, the states of affairs

have the same form. And what makes the configurations in these two states of affairs possible also makes configurations of the rest of the elements possible. That is, the states of affairs

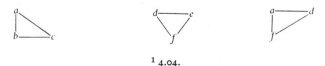

<hr />

[1] 4.04.

all have the same form. The form is, by definition, the possibility of the structure, and the possibility of the structure comes from the objects' all being of such a form that they can combine in this way. So, to put it roughly, the form of a state of affairs is the amalgam of the forms of the objects constituting it. I shall try to state this more clearly in the next chapter when I come to the picture theory, but I think that even now it should be clear, if what I say is right, why Wittgenstein wants to distinguish structure and form. In the fact which is a picture we can distinguish two classes of features: those which are necessary to the fact for it to picture what it pictures, and those which are conventional and might have been different. Recall the fact I mentioned before:

$$a\text{————————}b$$

and suppose we want to picture this. To object $a$ we give the name '$\alpha$' and to $b$ the name '$\beta$'; and we let the configuration:

$$\begin{array}{c} `\alpha' \\ \beta \end{array}$$

say that the objects are configured as in the fact above. Now we could have chosen a different configuration (structure); a picture must have *a* structure, but the structure it has is a matter of convention. So, the form-structure distinction marks the distinction (though this needs qualification) between the necessary and the conventional in a proposition and therefore between what in a proposition is philosophically important and what unimportant. The final justification of these claims, too, I must leave for the next chapter.

### 3. *Their Mutual Independence*

At 2.061–2 Wittgenstein makes his well-known claim:[1]

States of affairs are independent of one another.
    From the existence or non-existence of one state of affairs it is impossible to infer the existence or non-existence of another.

And what he says here for states of affairs he claims as well, *mutatis mutandis*, for elementary propositions; it is a mark of an elementary proposition that no other can contradict it.[2] 'Contradict' ('in

[1] See also 1.21, 4.27b.        [2] 4.211; see also 5.134.

Widerspruch stehen') should not, 2.062 suggests, be taken strictly; what Wittgenstein means is that no elementary proposition has a contrary. Now, states of affairs are configurations of objects, and as examples I have been taking spatial objects in spatial configurations. But now it seems that such examples are not states of affairs after all. Spatial configurations exclude one another; *a* and *b*'s being one inch apart, for example, means that they are not two, three, or four inches apart. Likewise, a proposition saying that *a* and *b* are an inch apart has as contraries the propositions which say they are two, three, or four. This is why I said earlier that the mutual independence of states of affairs and of elementary propositions is a puzzling affair. If things like this do not qualify, what will? On the face of it, the answer is either *nothing*, in which case Wittgenstein has simply failed to see how extreme the consequences of his claim were going to be, or *very little*, in which case it is hard to see how an entire language can be built out of such scanty resources—far scantier, certainly, than any other analyst of the period allowed himself.

The puzzle is solved, I think, in Wittgenstein's 1929 article, 'Some Remarks on Logical Form', which, like the *Investigations*, follows the rule that Wittgenstein's views are clearer in the recanting than the asserting:[1]

The mutual exclusion of unanalyzable statements of degree contradicts an opinion which was published by me several years ago and which necessitated that atomic propositions could not exclude one another. I here deliberately say 'exclude' and not 'contradict', for there is a difference between these two notions . . .

And Wittgenstein's acknowledging the difference makes it certain that his position is as extreme as I have just made out. But it would be best to preface his 1929 account with a quick review of and some speculations based upon a few of the conclusions from the last chapter. I argued there:

(1) That objects are particulars, and that the objects of space, for instance, are simple material things.

(2) That objects are unalterable in the sense that, just as in physics alteration is change in arrangement of simple particles,

[1] *LF* p. 168.

so in general alteration is change in the structure of objects.

(3) That property words disappear on analysis. Now, it is at 6.3751 that Wittgenstein gives his one example of the mutual exclusion of two situations, viz. the incompatibility of colours. The assertions that a point is red and that it is green cannot be true together; hence they are not elementary. This impossibility is logical; it is due, Wittgenstein explains to 'the logical structure of colour'. Now, in the previous chapter I also suggested what 'the logical structure of colour' might mean. In a sense, colours are given structure in optics. That is, classical optics reduces them to three primary colours, and any colour can be represented in a three dimensional co-ordinate system where each axis stands for one of the primary colours. In fact, if we adopted such a method of representation, then we could assign numerical values to all the shades on the basis of which they could be ranked in a variety of ways.[1] And atomic physics carries the reduction of colours even further than this, in that now each colour can be represented in terms of the position of particles in the surfaces of things. In this method of representation, too, colours form a system. In fact, on either representation, classical optics or atomic physics, the structure of two colours in virtue of which they stand internally related would be revealed.[2] Now, I think Wittgenstein may well have had this sort of consideration in mind when he made his remark about the incompatibility of colours, since he goes on in 6.3751 to consider:

... how this contradiction appears in physics: more or less as follows —a particle cannot have two velocities at the same time; that is to say, it cannot be in two places at the same time; that is to say, particles that are in different places at the same time cannot be identical.

My reading of 6.3751, which may at first seem too indebted to the sciences and not enough to logic, is reinforced, I think, by a late *Notebooks* entry, part of which I quoted in the previous chapter and all of which should be examined now:[3]

A point cannot be red and green at the same time: at first sight there seems no need for this to be a logical impossibility. But the very

---

[1] Cf. F. P. Ramsey: *The Foundations of Mathematics*, p. 213.
[2] See 4.123b.  [3] *Nbk.* 16.8.16.

language of physics reduces it to a kinetic impossibility. We see that there is a difference of structure between red and green.

And then physics arranges them in a series. And then we see how here the true structure of the objects is brought to light.

The fact that a particle cannot be in two places at the same time does look more like a logical impossibility.

If we ask why, for example, then straight away comes the thought: Well, we should call particles that were in two places different, and this in its turn all seems to follow from the structure of space and of particles.

(4) That a fact describable by use of a property-word is not on the simplest level of organization, for properties come into existence only with the configuration of objects. This view fits well with the construction I just put on 6.3751, because it suggests a familiar scientific process. I mean the process whereby a chemist analyses an ordinary language term (say, 'water') into elements ($H$ and $O$ in proportionate weights of $1 : 8$), and a physicist analyses these elements (say, the $H$ atom) into still more basic elements (a proton and a single electron). Now, this process of analysis in the natural sciences reminds one of *Tractatus* analysis in at least this one respect; in it too properties disappear. Water is cold or warm, red or green; atomic particles, almost by definition, are neither. I say 'almost by definition', because the elements of physics are bodies postulated, in part, in order to account for the temperatures and colours of macroscopic bodies.

(5) That Wittgenstein's thesis is a universal one: *all* properties disappear on analysis. Perhaps Wittgenstein intends his remarks on the incompatibility of colours to apply equally widely. That is, it may be part of his argument that for any property there is at least one other to which it stands in internal relation, which pair of properties logically exclude one another. Consider how this would work in the case of sounds. If we analyse in physical terms a statement to the effect that a sound is loud, it would reduce to statements about the motion of particles, to statements in wave mechanics. So would the statement that the sound is soft. What is important at present is that such analysis reveals the structure of the properties in virtue of which we speak of them as internally related, and that the elements figuring in the final analysis have themselves no degree of loudness. This is important, because if in

the final analysis no expression could stand in internal relation to another, then would it not seem that in the final analysis no proposition could exclude another?

But these are simply speculations, which the *Tractatus* says enough to prompt but does not, I believe, say enough to confirm or deny. I want now to turn to the 'Logical Form' article.

It begins with the familiar distinction between real and apparent form. In ordinary language we put into the same form (say the subject-predicate form) propositions whose real forms are quite different from one another. We know that they are different, because we analyse propositions, and analysis displays their real form:[1]

If, now, we try to get at an actual analysis, we find logical forms which have very little similarity with the norms of ordinary language. We meet with the forms of space and time with the whole manifold of spacial and temporal objects, as colours, sounds, &c., &c., with their gradations, continuous transitions, and combinations in various proportions, all of which we cannot seize by our ordinary means of expression.

Notice that in analysis we meet *the forms of space and time with the whole manifold of spatial and temporal objects*. So far as one can tell from the context, this remark is intended as a description of analysis in general. That is, analysis of propositions of whatever kind ends with statements about spatial and temporal (and perhaps other sorts of) objects. The expression 'the manifold of spacial and temporal objects', with its probably deliberate Kantian overtones, suggests that these spatial and temporal objects (among others perhaps) are, massed and structured, what constitute the world. Then, notice that we meet the manifold *as colours, sounds, &c., &c.* The manifold of objects appears to us in the form of colours, sounds, and so on; or, the other way around, colours, sounds, and the other things that we perceive are compositions of spatial and temporal objects. I single out these two remarks because they give some corroboration to a number of the claims I made in the last chapter: among others, that there are such things as temporal objects. Then, finally,—and this is the remark that I shall concentrate on now—notice that in analysis we meet with colours

[1] *LF* p. 165.

sounds, and so on, *with their gradations, continuous transitions, and combinations in various proportions.* Lengths, for example, can be one, two, three inches, &c.; that is, they can be arranged in gradations. Colours, as we see from a spectrum, are a continuous transition. And so forth. The full importance of this remark comes out in the illustration Wittgenstein gives of an actual analysis.[1] Suppose we want to describe a coloured patch in our visual field. Were we to superimpose a co-ordinate system of arbitrary scale upon our field of vision, we could describe the shape and position of the coloured patch by giving the co-ordinates of its boundaries. Wittgenstein's example is of a red patch *P*, as follows:

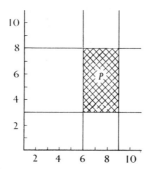

We can represent *P* by the expression '(6–9, 3–8)', and we can assert something of *P*, e.g. that it is red, with the symbol '(6–9, 3–8)*R*'. This is a *possible* way of symbolizing the fact that that *P* is red, but, as we know, not everything about it is *necessary* for symbolizing the fact. One would think that the numbers are not necessary. But the point Wittgenstein is making in this article is that sometimes numbers are necessary, even in fully analysed propositions. This opinion, he adds, is in contrast to what he believed earlier, presumably in the *Tractatus*. In the *Tractatus* he believed that any proposition which contained numbers was not fully analysed and that upon analysis the numbers would disappear. But numbers have to appear, he now thinks, in propositions describing *P*. More generally, they have to appear in propositions in which there occur properties which admit of gradation: that is, any property that has to do with 'gradations,

[1] *LF* pp. 165–6.

continuous transitions, and combinations in various proportions'. This includes, besides the length of an interval, properties like the pitch of a tone, the brightness or redness of a shade of colour, &c.[1] The situation is, in short, that in the *Tractatus* Wittgenstein thought that propositions involving properties which admitted of gradation were analysable into propositions which did not involve them, and that he now thinks that such propositions are not further analysable.

Wittgenstein has another, simpler example to explain his change of mind.[2] Take $b$ as the unit of brightness, and let '$E(b)$' say that an entity $E$ possesses this unit amount of brightness, let '$E(2b)$' say that it possesses twice the unit amount of brightness, and so on. What he thought in the *Tractatus*, Wittgenstein says, was that a statement like '$E(2b)$' could be analysed into the logical product '$E(b).E(b)$'. He has changed his mind, he says, because the analysis, no matter how amended, is not equivalent to the original proposition. The logical product '$E(b).E(b)$' says, not '$E(2b)$', but simply '$E(b)$', just as the logical product 'the sun is shining and the sun is shining' does not say more for the repetition. Wittgenstein, it appears, tried to find ways to remedy this difficulty, one of which he mentions. We could try to distinguish between the units of brightness; that is, we could analyse '$E(2b)$' into '$E(b').E(b'')$'. However, if we assume different units of brightness, then when an entity has only one unit the question could arise as to whether it is $b'$ or $b''$, which Wittgenstein rejects as absurd. Thus, he appears to be claiming: no patching of this analysis works; there is no other analysis; so, it has to be admitted that '$E(2b)$' is unanalysable.

How does this failure bear on logical independence? It is a characteristic of properties which admit of gradation:[3]

. . . that one degree of them excludes any other. One shade of colour cannot simultaneously have two different degrees of brightness or redness, a tone not two different strengths, &c. And the important point here is that these remarks do not express an experience but are in some sense tautologies.

Properties admitting of gradation logically exclude one another.

[1] *LF* p. 167.      [2] *LF* pp. 167–8.      [3] *LF* p. 167.

So when in the *Tractatus* Wittgenstein held that propositions involving such properties were analysable into propositions which did not, this was tantamount to holding that really elementary propositions could not exclude one another. '$E(b)$' says that $E$ has a unit amount of brightness, where it is left open whether it might not have more than this. And thus the only proposition that '$E(b)$' excludes is the proposition which denies that $E$ has any brightness at all, i.e. '$\sim E(b)$'. Such propositions, therefore, only exclude their negations, and, as we know, the negation of an elementary proposition is not itself elementary. Thus, when Wittgenstein changes his mind about '$E(2b)$' 's being analysable, he has also to change his mind about the independence of elementary propositions, as he confesses:[1]

I maintain that the statement which attributes a degree to a quality cannot further be analysed. .... The mutual exclusion of unanalyzable statements of degree contradicts an opinion which was published by me several years ago and which necessitated that atomic propositions could not exclude one another.

This gives the outline any proper account of logical independence will follow. But it leaves out some important details. For instance, it is not yet really clear what was so attractive about the idea to make Wittgenstein miss seeing its elementary flaw. Nor is it clear why the analysability of numbers was a matter of such importance. To start with the second question, it looks from the 'Logical Form' article as though a possible, perhaps even the preferred, method of representing most facts is with co-ordinate systems. Such a method of representation is the preferred one, apparently, for facts of colour, and procedure in certain sciences shows that it is at least a possible one for other kinds of facts. That is, many obvious cases of properties admitting of degree—temperatures, velocities, location, weights, and so forth—are representable this way. Perhaps, then, analysability of numbers is an important matter because in co-ordinate systems numbers appear essentially. And if Wittgenstein thinks that *all* properties of degree are representable this way, possibly even that they are most perspicuously represented this way, then the question as to whether

[1] *LF* p. 168.

elementary propositions exclude one another could be viewed simply as the question as to whether co-ordinate numbers can appear in fully analysed propositions. But I shall leave the matter here for the moment, because Wittgenstein's use of co-ordinate systems requires a discussion of its own, which will have to be postponed till later.[1]

Why was Wittgenstein so convinced of the analysability of numbers that he should have slipped up as he did? '. . . it would be surprising', he says in the 'Logical Form' article, 'if the actual phenomena had nothing more to teach us about their [i.e. simple propositions'] structure';[2] 'where ordinary language disguises logical structure', analysis reveals it.[3] Now, this is not much different from what he held in the *Tractatus*. He says in the *Tractatus* that if two propositions stand in any logical relation whatever, they do so in virtue of their structure.[4] Hence, that they are logically related will *show* when, upon analysis, their structure is revealed.[5] It follows from this that when two propositions are contraries, and where there is nothing about their structure to suggest such a relation, they cannot be fully analysed. For example, if two properties, $\phi$ and $\psi$, are mutually exclusive, this certainly does not show itself in the propositions '$\phi a$' and '$\psi a$'; so such propositions must be analysable. Take, for example, the propositions 'this is red' and 'this is green', said of the same object at the same time. Their analysis would involve, I have been suggesting, statements like those in physics, statements upon the position and velocity of particles. However, the analysis will not end here. The example of a physics-like statement I was using earlier, to put it in a slightly new form, was '$a\beta(3)$', which says that $a$ and $b$ are at three units distance from one another. This is the contrary of '$a\beta(2)$'. So, even these propositions contain structures which further analysis will reveal. The analysis Wittgenstein had in mind in the *Tractatus*, he admits in the 'Logical Form' article, was to write '$a\beta(3)$' as:

$$\text{`}a\beta.a\beta.a\beta\text{'}$$

and '$a\beta(2)$' as:

$$\text{`}a\beta.a\beta\text{'}$$

---

[1] See below and Ch. VIII.5.    [2] *LF* pp. 163–4.    [3] *LF* p. 163.
[4] 4.1211, 5.13, 5.2 *et seq.*; see this chapter, Sect. 2.    [5] 5.21.

And here mutual exclusion lies revealed in the propositional signs as clearly as (because rather like) the mutual exclusion of an object's extending from the beginning of a ruler placed aside it to the two-inch mark and its simultaneously extending to the three-inch mark. Thus, it appears that there were certain *a priori* considerations which led Wittgenstein to believe that an analysis of such propositions must be possible, no matter what practical difficulties might attach to its accomplishment. And these considerations are: (i) logical relations between propositions lie in their structure, and (ii) with analysis, structure is laid bare—in the strong sense just illustrated. That is, his fundamental thought seems to have been that propositions like '$\alpha\beta(3)$' and '$\alpha\beta(2)$' must be capable of analysis because, as their contrariety alone shows, there is more structure there to be revealed. Thus, elementary propositions will not have structures permitting logical relations; they can only contribute to the formation of those which have. Thus: (iii) if the truth of one proposition excludes the truth of another, they cannot be elementary, and vice versa. Apparently Wittgenstein was enough impressed by (i) and (ii) to accept (iii), in spite of difficulties in seeing how this analysis would actually work. It is a reassuring quality of an *a priori* demand that it can be met. I asked a short while ago how Wittgenstein could have made the mistake he did, and the most likely answer seems to me to be that he was convinced enough of these *a priori* considerations about analysis to be unconcerned with details of its execution.

Settling this question, as usual, raises others. I shall mention two. First, what is the significance of co-ordinate systems as a method of representing facts? I have already said that they seem to possess privileged status. One indication of this is Wittgenstein's describing the superimposition of a mesh on our visual field as 'the direction in which . . . the analysis of visual phenomena is to be looked for', and presumably he means visual phenomena in general. There is another, striking indication in the parallel to the 'Logical Form' example one finds at *Tractatus* 6.341.[1] Wittgenstein argues there that certain scientific laws are not themselves empirical, but rather are *a priori* intuitions of possible forms for

[1] See also 6.342; cf. *Nbk.* 6.12.14, 23.12.14.

those propositions in the sciences which are empirical.[1] And he gives an example of an *a priori* intuition of this sort and explains how it reduces the description of the world to a unified form. Consider a white surface covered with irregular black spots. Now, however these black spots are shaped or distributed I can describe them by superimposing a sufficiently fine square network and by saying of every square whether it is white or black. In this way, whatever the surface may be like, I reduce its description to a unified form. The illustration I have reproduced from the 'Logical Form' article would almost do as an illustration for 6.341.

This question leads on to a second. Wittgenstein's example of a colour statement, '$(6-9, 3-8)R$', is not fully analysed. Perhaps further analysis would follow the lines of this example from the *Tractatus*. Rather than speaking of the whole area $(6-9, 3-8)$, we should speak of each part our co-ordinate system defines. We should say what each is like, and the logical product of these statements would be equivalent to the original statement. This is not yet a full analysis, but it would look as if, no matter how far it went, the simplest individual we would talk about would be determined by the system we use, by the network we superimpose. Does this mean that what counts as an object is something *we* determine? Is the criterion of simplicity anthropocentric, so to speak? In a way it is so in mechanics; we speak of electrons, protons, neutrons, and so forth; they are the elements in the mesh we use at present. But there is no claim in physics that these particles are in a material sense simple, nor that the present mesh will not in future be replaced. Perhaps, too, Wittgenstein's proof of simples only proves there to be simples in this sense.[2] Yet before succumbing to this view of simplicity altogether, we should recall the burden of the 2.02's: that objects form the substance of the world, that they exist independently of what is the case, that they are unalterable. Does this not suggest that objects are simple in a material sense? At any rate, here is a central and as yet unresolved problem.

[1] See esp. 6.34.    [2] See also *Nbk.* 7.5.15b, 11.5.15b, 25.5.15a.

# VIII
# PICTURES

## 1. *The Picture Theory of Meaning*

FOR Wittgenstein, speaking of pictures is not just another way of speaking of propositional signs. The two are on different levels of generality: 'picture' the genus, and 'propositional sign' a species. Gramophone records and musical scores are pictures too;[1] phonetic spelling is a picture of spoken language.[2] Even things outside the range of the senses can be pictures; thoughts are pictures.[3] In fact, they are a good example of just how general a concept 'picture' is. Suppose we have a fact $p$. There will be an element in its propositional sign '$p$' for each element in $p$ and the arrangement of elements in '$p$' will say that the elements in $p$ are arranged as they are. Now, consider a person, $A$, thinking the fact $p$. Since a thought, too, is a picture, it must be that $A$'s thought consists of elements (as many as '$p$' had) and that these elements have an arrangement (as those in '$p$' did) which will say that the elements in $p$ are arranged as they are. This not only follows from Wittgenstein's saying that thoughts are pictures; he says it explicitly later in the *Tractatus*:[4]

... '$A$ believes that $p$', '$A$ has the thought $p$', and '$A$ says $p$' are of the form ' "$p$" says $p$': and this does not involve a correlation of a fact with an object, but rather the correlation of facts by means of the correlation of their objects.

Both '$A$ has the thought $p$' and ' "$p$" says $p$' assert, in effect, that there is a fact which has $n$ elements ($n$ being the number of elements in $p$) configured in a certain way, which configuration says that the $n$ elements in $p$ are arranged as they are. So, they both assert the existence of a relation between two facts: a picturing and a pictured fact; this is why they are of the same form. All that is special in the case of thinking is that here the picturing fact is a psychical fact composed of psychical elements. Now, exactly how different is a psychical fact from a propositional sign? This comes

---

[1] 4.011, 4.014.    [2] 4.011.    [3] 3; cf. 3.1, 3.5, 4.    [4] 5.542.

out more clearly in a passage from the *Notes Dictated to Moore*:[1]

The relation of 'I believe *p*' to '*p*' can be compared to the relation of
' "*p*" says *p*' to *p*: it is just as impossible that *I* should be simple as that
'*p*' should be.

*I* cannot be simple because my having this thought means that
in me, in the psychical part of me (Wittgenstein's word in the
*Tractatus* is 'Seele'), you can find a fact with the complexity
requisite for picturing *p*. The argument, in effect, is: *cogito, ergo
non simplex sum*: *I* am not simple, because *I* think, and thoughts are
pictures, and pictures are facts, and these picturing facts must
share the complexity of the facts they picture; thus, *I* consist,
among other things, of a number of psychical elements arranged
to make up picturing psychical facts. Can we know what these
psychical elements are like? Are they different from words?
Russell once asked Wittgenstein this in a letter. '. . . But a
*Gedanke*', Russell wrote, 'is a *Tatsache*: what are its constituents
and components, and what is their relation to those of the pictured
*Tatsache*?' To which Wittgenstein replied:[2]

I don't know *what* the constituents of a thought are but I know *that*
it must have such constituents which correspond to the words of
Language. Again the kind of relation of the constituents of the thought
and of the pictured fact is irrelevant. It would be a matter of psychology
to find out.

But, at any rate, does a thought consist of words? asked Russell:[3]

No! But of psychical constituents that have the same sort of relation to
reality as words. What those constituents are I don't know.

So when we consider pictures, we must think of them on a level of
generality which takes in thoughts and these unknown psychical
elements. What Wittgenstein has to say about the less general
matter of propositional signs and words he saves for the 3.1's,
and I shall leave till the next chapter.

The heart of the picture theory is pictorial form ('Form der
Abbildung'). Pictures are just as much facts as the facts they
picture, because pictures consists of elements combined in a

---

[1] *NM* 118.11–13.
[2] Letter 18: Cassino, 19.8.19, para. 2.                    [3] Ibid., para. 4.

definite way.[1] Thus, we can apply to pictures a distinction introduced earlier for facts generally: that between structure and form. The definite way in which its elements are combined is a picture's structure, and the possibility of its structure is its form.[2] To the form of, specifically, picturing facts Wittgenstein gives the name 'pictorial form'. Now, in order for one fact to be a picture of another, Wittgenstein tells us, it must have something identical with the fact it pictures,[3] namely, pictorial form.[4] Now, why must there be this identity? Indeed, why must there be any identity at all?

It is at 2.17 that Wittgenstein makes this claim, and following it at 2.171, he adds:

A picture can depict any reality whose form it has.

A spatial picture can depict anything spatial, a coloured one anything coloured, &c.

This remark has been taken to mean that the demand for identity in pictorial form results in a spatial fact's being depictable *only* by a spatial picture, a coloured fact's *only* by a coloured picture, &c. I think this cannot be right for at least three reasons. So far as I know, there is no argument in the *Tractatus* designed to show that ordinary language, deficient as it may be in some respects, does not picture the world. In fact, there is strong evidence to the contrary where Wittgenstein says that though at first sight a proposition, say as it stands on the printed page, does not seem to be a picture, it none the less is one.[5] And since ordinary propositions are not coloured, yet manage to depict coloured facts, it cannot be the case that only coloured pictures can depict coloured facts, spatial pictures spatial facts, &c. Then, secondly, even making no assumptions about the *Tractatus* attitude towards ordinary language, there is a parallel argument. Even in Wittgenstein's logically impeccable language we can, evidently, express our thoughts in propositions, that is: in words combined in a definite way,[6] or more specifically: in names the configuration of which says that the objects corresponding to the names are configured in a certain way.[7] So, again we have a picture which is

---

[1] 2.14, 2.141; cf. 3.14.  [2] 2.15b.  [3] 2.16, 2.161.  [4] 2.17; cf. 2.18.
[5] 4.011; see also 4.002c, d, e.  [6] 3.1 *et seq.*, esp. 3.14a.  [7] 3.2 *et seq.*, esp. 3.21.

spatial (the configuration of written signs)[1] which can depict anything that can be depicted: temporal, coloured, &c. Finally, thoughts are pictures, as we have just seen. Thoughts can be of (i.e. can depict) facts, be they spatial or temporal or coloured, &c. Yet we cannot say that a thought is a spatial fact, temporal fact, or coloured fact; in fact, as we saw in his reply to Russell, Wittgenstein does not know of what sorts of elements a thought consists and does not think he needs to know.

I mention these arguments because, if they are sound, then an ambiguity arises in the definition of pictorial form at 2.15b. Pictorial form, the definition says, is the possibility of the structure of the picture. Now, suppose my picturing fact is spatial while my pictured fact is temporal. My picturing fact, say, consists of two discs, standing for two events. I introduce a scale and a direction so that disc $\alpha$'s being so far in this direction from disc $\beta$ says that event $a$ occurred so long before event $b$, $\alpha$'s being so far in that direction says that $a$ occurred so much later, $\alpha$ and $\beta$'s being side-by-side says that the two events were simultaneous. Now, if the discs $\alpha$ and $\beta$ are considered simply as physical objects in their own right, then there are a number of possible combinations we have not yet considered: $\alpha$ can be on top of $\beta$, $\alpha$ and $\beta$ can be leaning against one another, &c. There are a number of combinations possible for $\alpha$ and $\beta$ other than those which make sense when $\alpha$ and $\beta$ are considered strictly as the representatives of $a$ and $b$. So, the definition at 2.15b may mean either: (i) pictorial form is the possibility of the structure of the picture simply as a fact in its own right, or (ii) it is the possibility of the structure of the picture not simply as a fact but as a picture. I mean by this second interpretation that when $\alpha$ and $\beta$ become the representatives of $a$ and $b$, they must also behave as regards combining as $a$ and $b$ behave. And thus it would make no sense to put disc $\alpha$ on top of disc $\beta$, or to have discs $\alpha$ and $\beta$ leaning against one another, &c. That is, the possible combinations of representatives of objects are restricted to the possible combinations of the objects they represent. This second, restrictive, interpretation is, I think, the proper one, because there is a second definition of pictorial form

[1] 3.11.

at 2.151 and its effect is to impose just this restriction. It goes:

Pictorial form is the possibility that things are related to one another in the same way as the elements of the picture.

So, when we speak of a picture's pictorial form we mean not only the possibility of its structure but also the possibility that the things in the fact are related in the same way as the elements of the picture. Or, rather, these two possibilities must amount to the same thing. This, however, could only be true if the picture's elements had the same possibility of combination as the fact's things; in other words, the restriction I have described would have to hold.

This restriction applies to the form of a picture. Yet I have said that this restriction means as well that the form of an element in a picture is restricted; an element must take on the same form as the object which it represents. The restriction on picture and on its elements, clearly, must amount to the same thing; one cannot limit the form of a fact, i.e. the possibility of the combination of its constituents (Def.), unless one limits the form of its constituents, i.e. the possibility of their combination in facts (Def.). Now, why must there be this restriction on either form? There is a possible answer to this in the pre-*Tractatus* writings. One finds in the *Notes on Logic*, as I pointed out in Chapter 11.3, the view that to give a symbol sense involves, at least in part, determining all the possible combinations the symbol will have. In terms of the case I have just been considering, what the *Notes* say is: to give one of these discs sense involves determining all of its possible combinations, i.e. determining its form. Now, either the form referred to is simply the form the disc has by being the object it is, or this form attaches to the disc in a different way. But we have already seen that the possibilities of combination for the disc need not be the same as the possibilities of combination of the object which it represents. Thus, we can have an object which functions as a representative entering combinations which make no sense when we regard that object as the representative. So, an object in its role as representative makes sense only when its possibilities of combination are restricted to those of the object it represents. Other than this it has no sense; one can say that it ceases to represent. From this suggestion in the *Notes on Logic* two important conclusions can be made to follow (and, I think, Wittgenstein makes follow), the first not very strictly and the second more strictly. First, a necessary condition for an element in a picture to have sense is that it take on the form of the object it represents. (I say *necessary* condition, because not only must we know through an element what form of object it represents but we must also know what particular object it is.) Then, second, the picturing fact must have the form of the fact it pictures, *because* the elements which make up the picture must take on the form of the objects that they represent. Thus, the necessity for identity in form between picture and fact is a necessity that gets in on this simpler level.

This second conclusion depends upon the first, which in turn depends upon the suggestion I have taken from the *Notes on Logic*. What evidence is there that in the *Tractatus* Wittgenstein accepts this suggestion? There is the weak evidence that, after all, it comes from his own earlier writings. Then, in the *Tractatus* itself there is this stronger evidence. Wittgenstein speaks of the pictorial relationship ('die abbildende Beziehung'), which, presumably, is the relation in which the picture stands to the fact.[1] It is said that the pictorial relationship is what makes one fact the *picture* of another fact.[2] Now, we know what this is: it is the pictorial form of the picture, i.e. it is that the picturing fact takes on the form of the fact it pictures. Then, Wittgenstein adds that the pictorial relationship consists of ('besteht aus') the co-ordinations of the elements of the picture and the things.[3] If it is the co-ordination of elements and things of which the pictorial relationship *consists*, then this co-ordination can only be, so far as I can see, a co-ordination in which the elements adopt the form of the objects. In no other way can such a co-ordination result in pictorial form. If this is so, then in the *Tractatus* Wittgenstein does indicate that the basis of pictorial form is the identity of form between element and object. Then, third, in support of this reading of the *Tractatus* there are entries in the *Notebooks*. The

[1] 2.1513.  [2] 2.1513.  [3] 2.1514.

logical connexion between names in a proposition, Wittgenstein writes:[1]

. . . must, of course, be one that is possible as between the things that the names are representatives of, and this will always be the case if the names really are representatives of the things.

We know, from the definition at 2.151, that the possibility that the names are combined in the proposition as are the things in the fact is pictorial form. What we are told here is that pictorial form is present when the names 'really are representatives of the things'. I take it that names *really* represent their things when they have more than just a one-to-one correlation with them, when, in other words, they also behave as regards combining as the things behave. This is a guess, but one borne out, I think, by other entries in the *Notebooks*, particularly this one:[2]

'*a*' can go proxy for *a* and '*b*' can go proxy for *b* when '*a*' stands in the relation '*R*' to '*b*': this is what that POTENTIAL internal relation that we are looking for consists in.

In general, names can represent things only so long as the names stand to one another in relationships (e.g. the relationship in the propositional sign '*aRb*') which are analogues to relationships that are possible for the things. Then, since the potential internal relation that Wittgenstein means here is the relation that holds between two facts when one pictures the other,[3] we once more reach the conclusion that picture and fact have pictorial form in common when their constituents have their forms in common.

To summarize these recent arguments: Wittgenstein demands that there be something identical between picture and fact, namely, pictorial form. What I have tried to prove is that the expanded version of this demand is: (i) an element in a picture, in order to be given sense, must, roughly speaking, be positioned in the symbolism in the same way as the object is positioned in reality (ii) because of this, a picture must consist of elements possessing the same forms as the elements of the pictured fact, (iii) therefore, it must have the same possibility of structure, i.e. the same pictorial

---

[1] *Nbk.* 4.11.14e.        [2] *Nbk.* 3.4.15c; see also 5.11.14d.
[3] See e.g. *Nbk.* 26.10.14a, 29.10.14e, 1.11.14 0, 25.4.15a, 26.4.15c.

form. Now, one trouble with my position, it may well be thought, is that it does not permit a difference in pictorial form between '$aRb$' and '$bRa$'. In fact, it does not even permit difference in pictorial form between '$aRb$' and '$aSb$'. This is not a consequence I wish to avoid, because it accords exactly with the way I defined 'form' in the previous chapter. The interpretation that I argued against there was that the form of a fact is what results from replacing constant elements in the fact with variable ones; I shall call this the 'variable-interpretation'. One of the things that counts against the variable-interpretation, I claimed, is that it conflicts with what Wittgenstein says about pictorial form. On the variable-interpretation, the fact $aRb$ would be said to have the following forms: $xRy$, $\phi(x, y)$, &c. I said that pictorial form could not be $xRy$, because a picturing fact does not have to be identical with the fact it pictures in all, configuration included, but its constituents; and that it could not be $\phi(x, y)$ either, because this would mean that picture and fact had only to have the same numerical multiplicity, and there is little doubt that Wittgenstein demands more than this. Pictorial form is somewhere between these two. So, the variable-interpretation needs alteration, and I think that the only alteration open to us leads straight to my interpretation. It would happen like this: we know a picture does not have to have the same constituents as its fact, nor even the same configuration; thus, to get its pictorial form we must let each of these vary, getting first $xRy$ and then $\phi(x, y)$. Yet this now gives the picture too much freedom. But each of these steps is necessary, so we cannot simply reverse them. Clearly, what we need is a way to modify them. The only way to do this is to say that, though the *elements* may vary, their *forms* must stay constant (which is exactly my position). It is the only way, because the only position between keeping the *particular* elements and *particular* configuration constant and letting them vary completely is keeping their *forms* constant. But it makes no sense to say the form *of the configuration* is kept constant; 'form of the configuration' has no meaning in the *Tractatus*. Thus, we have just one alternative; the forms of the elements must remain constant.

As for my having to say that '$aRb$' and '$bRa$' have the same pictorial form, there are separate grounds in the *Tractatus* for thinking they could not possibly have different ones. Let me drop the '*R*' and use '*ab*' and '*ba*' as my examples, where the configuration of the names now says what '*R*' said. Suppose '*ab*' says '*a* is higher than *b*'. Then, on the same convention, '*ba*' says '*b* is higher than *a*'. But it could, of course, have been the other way around: '*ba*' could, if we wished this to be the convention, say '*a* is higher than *b*'. Now, since pictorial form is what *must* be in common between two facts for the one to picture the other, both the facts '*ab*' and '*ba*' must have pictorial form in common with the fact that *a* is higher than *b*. Thus, since they have their pictorial form in common with the same fact, they have the same pictorial form.

## 2. *The Various Forms of Pictures*

So much for pictorial form. This still leaves the question: how, if at all, does pictorial form ('Form der Abbildung') differ from representational form ('Form der Darstellung')? And how do they differ from logical form ('logische Form'), that is, the form of reality ('Form der Wirklichkeit')? How, for example, are we to make sense of the following passage, in which all the various forms of pictures appear?[1]

A picture represents its subject from a position outside it. (Its standpoint is its representational form.) That is why a picture represents its subject correctly or incorrectly.

What any picture, of whatever form, must have in common with reality, in order to be able to depict it—correctly or incorrectly—in any way at all, is logical form, i.e. the form of reality.

A picture whose pictorial form is logical form is called a logical picture.

Every picture is *at the same time* a logical one. (On the other hand, not every picture is, for example, a spatial one.)

Logical pictures can depict the world.

Representational form, I believe, is sharply to be distinguished from pictorial form. A picture represents its object from outside it, Wittgenstein tells us, and its representational form is its standpoint. To depict something we must adopt a standpoint, and

[1] 2.173, 2.18, 2.181, 2.182, 2.19.

pictures of the same situation may differ because in making them we adopt different standpoints. The standpoint, in other words, is arbitrary. This is why a picture's representational form must be different from its pictorial form; the latter is never arbitrary. This also explains why it is through its representational form that a picture is true or false. By co-ordinating the elements of a picture with objects in a fact we give the elements reference and make possible combinations of them possible bearers of sense. But it is not until we choose a standpoint—that is, determine that *this* structure of the elements will be used to say that the objects are structured in *that* way—that the picture can be true or false. Put roughly, a picture's pictorial form has to do with its having *sense*, and its representational form with its being *true or false*. I base these claims not only on the definition of representational form, which is quite short, but on other remarks as well. As we know, Wittgenstein speaks in the 2.1's of a pictorial relationship ('die abbildende Beziehung'). We discover later, at 4.462b, that there is also a representing relationship ('die darstellende Beziehung'). Wittgenstein explains that a proposition's representing relations are its conditions of agreement with the world. Well, certainly the co-ordinations of elements and objects, of which the pictorial relation consists, are not that. To get a picture's conditions of agreement we must take the additional step of setting up a relation between a configuration of the elements and the configuration of the objects. Then, further remarks along the same lines are to be found in the *Notebooks*. At the time of the *Notebooks* Wittgenstein did not have the name 'pictorial form', though he obviously had the concept.[1] So the two forms are not contrasted by name. Wittgenstein does, though, use the term 'representation'. He speaks of 'principles of representation'[2] ('Prinzipe der Darstellung') and of a 'way of representing'[3] ('Darstellungsweise') and, what is clearly the same thing, of a 'method of representing'[4] ('Darstellungsmethode') and even of the 'representing relationship'[5] ('darstellende Beziehung' or 'darstellende Relation');

---

[1] See e.g. *Nbk.* 20.10.14b; for use of 'logical form' see e.g. 25.4.15a.
[2] *Nbk.* 1.11.14n.
[3] *Nbk.* 30.10.14e, f, i; 31.10.14b–e; 3.11.14 0; cf. *PI* paras. 50, 104.
[4] *Nbk.* 30.10.14c.  [5] *Nbk.* 1.11.14a; 2.11.14a; 3.11.14b, f.

and he also says that pictures 'represent'[1] ('darstellen') their facts. What he says with this terminology I will put as much as possible in his own words. When he mentions logical form (which, I shall soon argue, is equivalent to pictorial form), he says:[2]

The logical form of the proposition must already be given by the forms of its component parts. (And these have to do only with the *sense* of the propositions, not with their truth or falsehood).

If pictorial form does not have to do with truth or falsity, what, according to the *Notebooks*, does?[3]

The picture has whatever relation to reality it does have. And the point is how it is supposed to represent ['darstellen']. The same picture will agree or fail to agree with reality according to how it is supposed to represent ['darstellen'].

Thus, truth and falsity come into consideration when the method of representing has been determined. Before then, the same picture, say '*ab*', can depict a number of states of affairs—even when '*a*' and '*b*' are thought of as signs already having meaning. What more we have to do is determine what one state of affairs this one configuration of the signs, '*ab*', shall picture. When this is done, when its method of representing has been determined, then we can consider whether the picture is true or false. Wittgenstein makes this same point again and again; let me give just one more version of it. Though the truth or falsity of a picture is something which has to appear, as it were, subsequent to the picture, still one must:[4]

. . . know in advance *how* it will appear.

And this is to say that one must know what 'Darstellungsweise' has been used, because:[5]

The way of representing ['Darstellungweise'] determines how the reality has to be compared with the picture.

Once we understand the difference between pictorial and representational forms we can see, I think, the point of logical

---

[1] *Nbk.* 30.10.14b; 1.11.14h, n; 3.11.14j, p; 5.11.14d, e.
[2] *Nbk.* 1.11.14f; see also g.     [3] *Nbk.* 1.11.14h.
[4] *Nbk.* 1.11.14 l–m.     [5] *Nbk.* 31.10.14e.

form, i.e. the form of reality. The language of 2.17 and 2.18
makes it clear that pictorial form and logical form are the same;
they are that which must be common to a fact and its picture,
which, as we know, is the form of the fact. This, I think, is why
Wittgenstein calls it the form of reality. It is the form of that
part of reality corresponding to the picture. Wittgenstein also
calls it 'logical' form, perhaps, to distinguish it from structure; a
picture does not have to have the same configuration as the fact it
pictures (configuration, one might say, is one of the matters of
fact about the fact), but only its form, as defined at 2.033 (which is
a logical feature of the fact). Now, since pictorial form is the same
as logical form, pictures, Wittgenstein says, are logical pictures.
That is, we may choose as the representational form for our
picture a fact which already has the form of the fact we are
picturing: say a spatial fact for a spatial fact. On the other hand, we
can choose, say, a temporal fact to picture this same spatial fact,
in something of a reversal of the example I used earlier with the
discs. But in this case, as we know, the temporal fact must adopt
the form of the spatial fact being pictured. So, either way, naturally or by adoption, the picturing fact will have the form of the
pictured fact, that is, logical form. So, either way, the picture can
be called a logical picture. However, not every picture is, say,
spatial. Being spatial is for a picture only its representational form,
and the choice of a representational form is arbitrary. Even if the
fact to be pictured is spatial, a temporal fact will do as well for its
picture as another spatial fact. This is why Wittgenstein ends with
the comment: logical pictures *can* depict the world. We need not
have the representational form the same as the form of the fact;
*logical* pictures do perfectly well.

3. *Interim Summary*

As precisely as possible, then, what is the point of the picture
theory? If we look closely at the start of the 2.1's we see that
Wittgenstein sets out one by one the characteristics of models and
pictures which, he thinks, propositional signs, thoughts, &c. have
too. (i) To each object in the fact there corresponds an element in
the picture, and vice versa; that is, there is a one-to-one relation

between constituents in facts and their pictures.[1] (ii) A picture consists in the fact that its elements are arranged in a definite way; thoughts, propositional signs, &c., as much as models, are facts in their own right.[2] (iii) The arrangement of the elements in the picture says that the elements in the fact are arranged in such-and-such a way; it is the arrangement in the picture that corresponds to the arrangement in the fact.[3] (iv) The elements in the picture can only combine with one another in ways possible for the objects.[4] Regarding this last point, the picture theory is supposed to have been suggested to Wittgenstein by a courtroom model of an automobile accident:[5]

In the proposition a world is as it were put together experimentally. (As when in the law-court in Paris a motor-car accident is represented by means of dolls, &c.)

A doll and a little automobile can be put in a number of relations to one another, but all of them will also be possible for the real things. Even this characteristic a propositional sign has. Because even though, when we write or speak of an automobile accident, the elements we are using are not little automobiles and dolls, pictorial form guarantees that they will behave as if they were. It is this last feature in particular, I believe, which leads Wittgenstein to conclude that a propositional sign is little short of a *tableau vivant*.[6]

## 4. *Hertz and the Picture Theory*

The picture theory comes almost in its entirety from Hertz. Wittgenstein was first, perhaps, to apply a picture theory of meaning to the whole of language, but not first to apply it to a part.

Wittgenstein begins his picture theory with the assertion: 'Wir machen uns Bilder der Tatsachen.'[7] Hertz on the first page of the Introduction to *The Principles of Mechanics* says: 'Wir machen uns innere Scheinbilder oder Symbole der äusseren Gegenstände'; (here Hertz speaks of 'Scheinbilder', but the word he more

---

[1] 2.13, 2.131.     [2] 2.14, 2.141.     [3] 2.15.     [4] 2.151.
[5] *Nbk.* 29.9.14b; see Malcolm: *Ludwig Wittgenstein: A Memoir*, pp. 68–69; cf. 3.1431, *NL* II 12–13.
[6] 4.0311.     [7] 2.1

normally uses is 'Bilder'). Wittgenstein says that there must be
something common between picture and fact;[1] or, as Hertz puts it,
'there must be a certain conformity between nature and our
thought'.[2] There must be conformity because, according to
Wittgenstein, our names must behave as regards combining as
the objects in nature behave,[3] or, according to Hertz, because 'the
form which we give [pictures] is such that the necessary consequents of the pictures ['Bilder'] in thought are always the
pictures ['Bilder'] of the necessary consequents in nature of the
things pictured'.[4] What are the things that, according to Wittgenstein and Hertz, pictures must share with their facts?[5] Among
others, Wittgenstein says, a picture must have the same numerical
multiplicity as its fact;[6] and Hertz says that a system that is the
model of another must satisfy the condition 'that the number of
co-ordinates of the first system is equal to the number of the
second'.[7] In fact, the logical isomorphism between picture and
fact must be such that, as Wittgenstein says, the gramophone
record, the musical idea, the score, the sound-waves stand to one
another in the same pictorial relation which holds between
language and the world;[8] or, as Hertz says, 'If one system is a
model of a second, then, conversely, the second is also a model of
the first' and 'If two systems are models of a third system, then
each of these systems is also a model of the other.'[9] Even the
thoughts in our heads are pictures; so they too must stand in this
internal relation;[10] 'the relation of a dynamical model', Hertz says,
'to the system of which it is regarded as the model, is precisely the
same as the relation of the images which our mind forms of things
to the things themselves'.[11] For example, the relation between $A$'s
thought that $p$ and $p$ itself is comparable to the relation between
'$p$', the proposition, and $p$;[12] or in Hertz's version 'the agreement

---

[1] 2.16, 2.161.        [2] Hertz: *The Principles of Mechanics*, p. 1.
[3] 2.151, 2.17.        [4] Op. cit., p. 1.
[5] For Wittgenstein's full answer see 2.1's *passim*; for Hertz's see op. cit.,
pp. 1–3 *passim*.
[6] See 4.04b.
[7] Op. cit., para. 418; see also p. 2 (picture must be 'correct') and p. 10 (explanation of correctness).
[8] 4.014, 4.0141.        [9] Op. cit., para. 419.        [10] 3, 3.02; cf. *Nbk.* 12.9.16.
[11] Op. cit., para. 428.        [12] 5.542.

between mind and nature may therefore be likened to the agreement between two systems which are models of one another . . .'.[1] Now the simplest thing with which we need deal in pictures or models are what Wittgenstein calls 'objects' and Hertz 'material particles' or 'material points'. Objects, we know, are eternal[2]— in *Philosophical Investigations* Wittgenstein says they are 'what cannot be destroyed';[3] and material particles, Hertz tells us, are 'invariable and indestructible'.[4] A system (a body), according to Hertz, is an aggregate of these material points,[5] which may explain even the language of Wittgenstein's remark in the *Notebooks* that analysis into simple components can be thought of as the division of a body into material points.[6] The world is, if not entirely then partly, an aggregate of material points. The models, the pictures, we make of the world are built in a similar way out of the symbols which represent these material points.

Now, we may distinguish, says Wittgenstein, between a pictorial form ('Form der Abbildung'), which must be common to a fact and its picture, and a representational form ('Form der Darstellung'), which, being a matter of convention, may vary between pictures of the same fact. In outline, this distinction too is in Hertz. In another work, *Electric Waves*, he examines the way a single phenomenon lends itself to explanation in apparently different theories. He says of this:[7]

But scientific accuracy requires of us that we should in no wise confuse the simple and homely, as it is presented to us by nature, with the gay garment which we use to clothe it. Of our own free will we can make no change whatever in the form of the one, but the cut and colour of the other we can choose as we please.

In particular, he is concerned with the existence of three different 'representations' ('Darstellungen') of Maxwell's theory, and with discovering the 'fundamental conceptions' behind them:[8]

. . . the representation ['Darstellung'] of the theory in Maxwell's own work, its representation as a limiting case of Helmholtz's theory, and its representation in the present dissertations—however different in form

---

[1] Op. cit., para. 428.  [2] 2.027, 2.0271.  [3] *PI* para. 59.
[4] Op. cit., para. 3.  [5] Op. cit., paras. 9–11.  [6] *Nbk.* 20.6.15m.
[7] Hertz: *Electric Waves*, p. 28.  [8] Op. cit., p. 21.

['Formen']—have substantially the same inner significance. This common significance of the different modes of representation ['verschiedenen Formen'] . . ., and not Maxwell's peculiar conceptions or methods, would I designate as 'Maxwell's theory' . . . Maxwell's theory is Maxwell's system of equations. Every theory which leads to the same system of equations, and therefore comprises the same possible phenomena, I would consider as being a form or special case of Maxwell's theory . . .

Now, as Wittgenstein points out, this practice of symbolizing the same thing in different ways and different things in the same way is a source of much confusion.[1] Or, as Hertz remarks:[2]

The very fact that different modes of representation contain what is substantially the same thing, renders the proper understanding of any one of them all the more difficult. Ideas and conceptions which are akin and yet different may be symbolised in the same way in the different modes of representation.

The theme Hertz is developing in these last remarks is by now familiar. It is found in the section of the *Tractatus* devoted to scientific language. It recurs in writings of several men, who acknowledge themselves in this regard to be Wittgenstein's followers: Ramsey, Schlick, slightly later Watson, and most recently Toulmin.[3] I think enough has been cited in Hertz to show a parallel with the *Tractatus* picture theory. I want now to turn to the subject of scientific language. For in this way you will see how central a place Hertz's version of the picture theory—that is, roughly, a picture theory confined to scientific discourse—occupied in Wittgenstein's thinking. And you will also find, I think, that in this version the picture theory is at its most persuasive and Wittgenstein's intentions are at their clearest.

## 5. *The Language of the Sciences*

The 6.3's are Wittgenstein's examination of the logical status of scientific propositions. One of his chief points is that many general statements in science need not be treated as truth-functions of

---

[1] 3.32–3.324.          [2] Op. cit., p. 21.
[3] F. P. Ramsey: *The Foundations of Mathematics*, M. Schlick: 'Causality in Contemporary Physics', W. H. Watson: *On Understanding Physics*, S. Toulmin: *The Philosophy of Science*.

elementary propositions. They are not empirical, so not strictly propositions; they are, rather, recommendations of a method for representing a certain class of phenomena uniformly and concisely. It is here that the illustration of a white surface with irregular black spots makes its appearance: we may describe the spots by superimposing a sufficiently fine square network and reporting of each square whether it is white or black.[1] The only empirical statements we can make in a system like this will be either reports made by using the language the system provides or, perhaps, reports to the effect that the particular fineness involved in the language is or is not effective in describing this particular surface. Now, Wittgenstein's point is that many scientific laws are like the mesh in this illustration. Their function is not to make reports, not even very general ones, but to supply representational techniques by which reports can be made. Thus, when this kind of law is superseded, it is not, for it cannot be, falsified. What happens is that a better method of representation is found. Perhaps it is illustration, possibly it is even verification, of this thesis that in general we do not say of Einstein's work that it proved Newton's wrong; in fact, it is only under certain circumstances that Einstein's language is definitely to be preferred. On this view, what Einstein did was to discover a new representational form, to present a finer grid.

This ubiquitous grid example seems also to lie at the bottom of Wittgenstein's metaphor about logical space. The essence of the metaphor is, I think, comparison of a sentence with a point in a co-ordinate system, and so names with single co-ordinate numbers.[2] In a given co-ordinate system putting two numbers together defines a point; in a given language putting two names together makes a statement. In this way, languages are a kind of logical co-ordinate system. And as there are different co-ordinate systems as a result of choosing different points of origin, different scales, and so forth, there are different representational forms in language.[3] Now, from these roots all the rest of the metaphor grows. If two names are of forms permitting combination, their combination is logically all right; it would be as impossible for a

[1] 6.341.   [2] See *Nbk.* 29.10.14e–f.   [3] See *Nbk.* 30.10.14c–d.

conjunction of names to contradict logic as for a pair of co-ordinates to contradict geometry.[1] A conjunction will always determine
a 'logical place' ('logischer Ort').[2] Furthermore, as in geometry to
specify one set of co-ordinates involves the whole apparatus of
grid, point of origin, and so on, so the determination of one logical
place brings along with it a whole symbolism with all its rules and
operations—or, as Wittgenstein puts it, the logical scaffolding will
already be given by it.[3] There is a logical place corresponding to
every state of affairs. And facts, i.e. existent states of affairs,
when put together, constitute the world,[4] just as all points in a
plane which are occupied, when put together, constitute a geometrical figure, the sort which in 6.341 stands for the world which
is to be described.

What is to be made of this recurrent picture? I mentioned a body
of *Tractatus*-influenced writings on the nature of scientific
language, and I think the answer is to be found in an argument
which runs through them. In stating this argument now I am
going to make these authors look far more like one another than in
fact they do, because it is only a certain point of agreement
between them that need concern us.

A scientific theory, the argument runs, can be described 'simply
as a language for discussing the facts the theory is said to explain'
(Ramsey).[5] Hence, 'when we assert a causal law we are asserting
a variable hypothetical which is not strictly a proposition at all,
but a formula from which we derive propositions' (Ramsey).[6]
'A law of nature', to repeat, 'does not have the logical character
of a "proposition" but represents "a direction for the formulation
of propositions"' (Schlick).[7] This is so because adopting a law is
choosing a way of talking about facts. The laws of mechanics,
for example, 'are the laws of our method of representing mechanical phenomena, and . . . since we actually choose a method of

---

[1] 3.032; see also 3.4 (cf. *Nbk.* 1.11.14t), 3.411 (cf. *Nbk.* 7.11.14).

[2] 3.4 (cf. *Nbk.* 1.11.14s); see also 3.41 (cf. *Nbk.* 7.11.14–19.11.14), 4.0641
(cf. *Nbk.* 3.11.14r–v, 6.11.14b, 9.11.14e–f, 24.11.14e).

[3] See 3.42 (cf. *Nbk.* 23.11.14, 15.12.14b, 16.12.14); see also 4.023e (cf. *Nbk.*
20.10.14h), 6.124.

[4] See 1.13; see also 2.013, 2.11, 2.202.

[5] Op. cit., p. 212.        [6] Op. cit., p. 251.

[7] Op. cit., p. 190; see also pp. 285–6; cf. Toulmin: op. cit., pp. 69–70, 86–87.

representation when we describe the world, it cannot be that the
laws of our method say anything about the world' (Watson).[1] Now,
different methods of representing the same phenomenon cannot
themselves be totally unalike. Since they must have something in
common with what they represent, they will have something in
common with one another. 'Two methods of representing the
same phenomena must agree in some way. . . . What is common to
the two pictures by the different methods of representing is like
what is common to two photographs of the same scene printed
from half-tone blocks with differing screen mesh' (Watson).[2]
What then makes us choose between two methods of representation, if not truth and falsity? At the time these authors were writing
the important case, I suspect, was the one I just alluded to: Einstein's theories supplanting Newton's. First of all, what Einstein's
work did was to account 'for some limits, which had hitherto been
unexplained, to the accuracy with which Newton's mechanics
can be used to calculate the motions of the planets; but it superseded Newton's mechanics only for the most refined theoretical
purposes, and could only whimsically be said to prove the older
laws of motion untrue' (Toulmin).[3] So, 'it is not a matter of
Newton's laws being wrong and Einstein's being right. In many
cases our experiments do not yield pictures of grain fine enough to
represent what the relativist asserts should be the case. For such
pictures Newton's laws are quite exact. . . . The fact is that in
physics we choose the particular method of representation adequate to the purpose in mind' (Watson).[4] To generalize, then, a
physical theory 'is not true or false but is good or bad, useful or
useless' (Schlick),[5] and 'the word "correct" as applied to a physical
theory has to be understood as "correct relative to a certain degree
of fineness of the observations" ' (Watson).[6] Also, we generally
think of 'a method which gives correctly the possibility of representing nature with greater detail than another . . . as the better
method—and it is so when it is a question of showing detail.
We think of the second method as an approximation to the first.
We tend, therefore, to arrange methods in a series according to the

[1] Op. cit., p. 52.  [2] Op. cit., p. 43.  [3] Op. cit., p. 70.
[4] Op. cit., p. 44.  [5] Op. cit., p. 285.  [6] Op. cit., p. 63.

degree of fineness of the pictures of phenomena that can be made
by means of them, and of course from this point of view the last
member of the series is the best' (Watson).[1]

An example will make all this clearer. Toulmin gives the most
detailed: how 'the geometrical method of representation in optics'
is superseded by the wave-theory of light, a 'technique of representation' of greater 'refinement';[2] he likens the first to a crude
road map, the second to a detailed physical map, providing in the
process the fullest exposition in my acquaintance of Wittgenstein's
analogy of theories and maps.[3] But the example I shall consider is
a more concise one of Watson's.[4] He is interested in methods for
describing the motion of particles. He considers the motion of a
spot projected on to a screen from a cinema film. Suppose the
film moves at twenty frames per second, the frames separated, of
course, by brief intervals of darkness. The motion of the dot looks
continuous. Hence, it is reasonable for us to superimpose a simple
co-ordinate system and to represent the path by $x=f(t)$, $y=g(t)$,
where $f$ and $g$ are continuous functions. But then suppose certain
evidence, made possible, say, by new techniques of observation,
suggests that there are times when there is no spot at all on the
screen, and others when the spot is stationary. That is, the motion
now seems to us to be discontinuous. We want to represent this
discontinuity; yet suppose it is convenient for us to preserve the
continuous representation, that is, the unbroken line on the graph
marking the spot's path. We can do this by altering the form of
$f(t)$ and $g(t)$ so as to allow the spot to be motionless for the short
intervals it is visible, and then by postulating continuous motion
during the dark intervals. As Watson concludes, 'these two
methods—continuous and discontinuous—are equally allowable
methods of representing the motion, but one is likely to regard the
latter as the more appropriate and less artificial method'.[5] This
example is not entirely factitious; it has bearings, which Watson
later considers, on the motion of atomic particles. And his point
here is that two different laws can be formulated for motion of this

[1] Op. cit., p. 50.          [2] Op. cit., *passim*, but esp. Ch. 4.
[3] See also Watson: op. cit., esp. pp. 105 *et seq.*, but also pp. 52, 61–62, 89–90.
[4] Op. cit., pp. 85–86.          [5] Op. cit., p. 86.

sort, one with the continuous and the other with the discontinuous functions; and that neither of these laws should be thought of as making a claim about the world; and, finally, that the grounds for their evaluation are not truth and falsity but such considerations as artificiality, crudity, and notational convenience.

This should make Wittgenstein's notion of representational form clearer. However, I introduced these *Tractatus*-influenced writings with the promise that they would explain the recurrent grids in Wittgenstein's work, and it is this other side of Watson's example I must now explore. A co-ordinate system is, doubtlessly, an important piece of symbolism in the sciences. Here it is used to record a body's motion. It can also record, say, the ratio of mass to volume. On one-dimensional scales temperatures can be plotted. Watson calls these one-, two-, &c., dimensional scales 'spaces of representation'.[1] There is a space corresponding to each property, so that it is possible to speak of a motion space, temperature space, colour space, and so on.[2] Suppose we want to represent an object that changes colour. We would need two spaces: one for colour and one for time. If we wished, further, to represent its shape, we would need yet another space of at least two dimensions.[3] In this fashion an object may be represented, Watson says, as a set of the spaces of each of its properties. But it would be better to use Watson's own words at this point, for they will interest a *Tractatus* reader:[4]

To say that a thing has a certain property means that the thing occupies a place in the corresponding space. We cannot think of the thing apart from this possibility. A thing has geometrical form and has a place in the space of each property, so when we speak of the substance of which the thing is made we have in mind that the appropriate places in the property spaces are occupied while the geometrical form is left variable. We can therefore represent a substance by the proper point in the multi-dimensional space which is the product of the property spaces.

I think we are entitled to conclude now, that Wittgenstein too must have held that many, perhaps all, properties were representable in *n*-dimensional scales, and that this sort of representation must have been very much at the front of his mind when

[1] Op. cit., p. 100.    [2] Op. cit., pp. 100–1.    [3] Op. cit., p. 103.
[4] Op. cit., p. 101.

he contrived the picture theory. I think that, considering how Wittgenstein thought of analysis, we might even go further and conclude that a stage in all reduction involves statements akin to those in the physical sciences, and that such statements are best expressed in $n$-dimensional scales. That is, not only are properties expressible in such scales, they are most perspicuously expressed that way. Most perspicuously, because in, say, certain propositions in physics the numerical multiplicity of the elements in the propositions begins to mirror the multiplicity of the facts, and their real, in contrast to their grammatical, form starts to appear. And the best expression for these propositions, it has been found, is in numerical scales. This stronger hypothesis would explain a lot. It would explain straightforwardly the *Tractatus* reference to a colour space, tone space, and so on.[1] It would account for both the naturalness and prevalence of the logical space metaphor.[2] And, as I mentioned in the last chapter, it would show why the analysability of numbers is so central an issue in the 'Logical Form' article. In fact, I believe the stronger conclusion is probably the right one, both because of its explanatory value and because of the circumstantial evidence these writings, especially Watson's, provide.

## 6. *Final Summary*

I do not take it as my job to *evaluate* either this important thesis about the character of scientific laws or the version of the picture theory it contains. I admitted already that this truncated version of the picture theory seems to me to show it at its best. All I wish to add to this is a recommendation: namely, that anyone who does take on the job of evaluating the picture theory should give this version of it far more attention than it has yet received.

I have two points in summary. First, I think the last two sections show something important about the development of the picture theory. The theory formulated with specific reference to scientific language is the version of the theory Wittgenstein found in Hertz and the version which years after the *Tractatus* he was passing on to pupils and colleagues. It is reasonable, therefore, to

[1] 2.0131b.     [2] See esp. 1.13, 2.013, 2.11, 2.202.

call it the core version of the picture theory. Between these two periods, in the *Tractatus* itself, Wittgenstein expanded the core version into a theory of meaning generally. Accordingly, we might look at the *Tractatus* picture theory—and I think this is the correct way to look at it—as being the recommendation that scientific language be the model for all language. Wittgenstein does say that the totality of true significant propositions is the complete natural science.[1] On this reading, he would also say that certain fairly obvious features of scientific discourse—for example, that one has a choice of representational techniques, that one builds models of the world, that these models contain one item for each one in what is being modelled—show what is essential in language generally. That is, these are features of ordinary discourse; if not of the sentences we normally use, then of the elementary sentences underlying them.

I imply with this last remark that, though some picture theories may not require a logical atomism, Wittgenstein's does. This is the second subject I want to consider. Precisely how are Wittgenstein's picture theory and his atomism related? And what, if anything, does the picture theory reveal about the atomism? The last section might well be taken as demonstration that they are quite independent of one another, since many wheels of a picture theory were turning there without the help of any atomistic machinery. It would be a complicated job to state, in general, exactly what claims a picture theory would have to make, or just how wide in scope it would have to be, before it necessarily involved logical atomism. I suspect that, if we did this, and if we paid attention to the differences between the authors I have been lumping together, we would find commitment to atomistic doctrines of quite different degrees: with Hertz a great deal, with the rest little or none. However, the general problem aside, the case of the *Tractatus* can, I believe, be settled with less difficulty. We need consider only one of Wittgenstein's grounds for saying that propositions are pictures. He claims that there is an element in a proposition for each element in the corresponding fact. A proposition of the form '$\phi a$'—say, 'this is red'—quite clearly does

[1] 4.11.

not have one element for each one in the fact. This is not the case until elementary propositions are reached. But '$\phi a$' is a picture, because it can be analysed into a form where it will correspond to its fact element for element, and where its arrangement will model the arrangement of the fact. Thus, when Wittgenstein says that though a proposition set out on the printed page may not look like a picture none the less it is one,[1] he means, in effect, that the proposition can be reduced to elementary propositions which *are* pictures. I do not mean that only elementary propositions are pictures, because this is obviously not what Wittgenstein says;[2] all significant propositions are pictures. But elementary propositions are the primary pictures, in the sense that it is by virtue of the elementary propositions which compose them that complex propositions are pictures.[3]

Thus, it is because the *Tractatus* is a theory of logical atomism that it has the picture theory of meaning it does have. It would be unsurprising, therefore, for the picture theory to show something about the atomism. One thing worth noticing is that in the one type of example we have of the picture theory at work, it has nothing to do with sense-data. It could not, one might feel, be further away: it has to do with the description of the world, as we have it in science. And it seems likely that the models Wittgenstein talks about in the *Tractatus* are akin to the models Hertz talks about in *The Principles of Mechanics*; each asserts that what we do in language generally (Wittgenstein) or in the language of mechanics (Hertz) is to make models of reality. Wittgenstein's models, then, can be understood in the ordinary sense of the word; propositions reconstruct states of affairs in much the way that an accident is reconstructed in a courtroom or in the way a physicist constructs a dynamical system on paper.[4] That is, in each case what we are modelling are states of affairs, the existence of which, by definition, constitutes reality. Of course, if read this way, the picture theory reinforces the views I have been offering of Wittgenstein's

[1] 4.011.
[2] See 2.11 (note plural 'Sachverhalte'), 2.203 ('Sachlage', not 'Sachverhalt', is used), 3 (note plural 'Tatsachen'), 4.011 (which says that ordinary propositions, presumably not elementary, are pictures), &c.
[3] Cf. *Nbk.* 31.10.14f.          [4] See 4.04b.

atomism. And so, in the end, I shall argue it does. For the moment I will leave the argument on this hypothetical note. One can still find grounds for doubt. To mention one, Wittgenstein clearly intends his description of language to be extraordinarily general. So perhaps he himself would read the *Tractatus* in a realist way, but perhaps at the same time he would be willing to have it read in a sense-datum way. I think not. But I have not yet shown it, and that argument must wait till later.

# IX

# THOUGHTS

## 1. Wittgenstein's Theory of Judgement

No one any longer feels that a philosophical position is incomplete without its 'theory of judgement'. The heyday for this idea was from the 1880's to the 1920's, from Bradley's *Principles of Logic* to Wittgenstein's *Tractatus*. I should certainly say the idea survives in the *Tractatus*. The 3.0's, I should say, are Wittgenstein's own theory of judgement, and there are a number of propositions later in the *Tractatus* that can only be understood in connexion with someone's, usually Russell's or Frege's, theory of judgement.[1] At first, in the 1880's and 1890's, there were two lines of development: one beginning with Bradley and his crusade to lead England out of the 'psychological attitude' in which it had 'lived too long',[2] developed by Bosanquet,[3] and purged of its still lingering psychologism by Moore;[4] the other coming from Frege, rather as a philosophical by-product of his researches into the foundations of mathematics.[5] These two lines met at Russell,[6] and, as I shall try to show, from him ran on together to Wittgenstein.

In *Principia Mathematica* Russell gave this concise statement of his theory of judgement:[7]

Let us consider a complex object composed of two parts *a* and *b* standing to each other in the relation *R*. The complex object '*a*-in-the-relation-*R*-to-*b*' may be capable of being perceived; when perceived it is perceived as one object. Attention may show that it is complex; we then *judge* that *a* and *b* stand in the relation *R*. . . . This judgement of

---

[1] 4.064, 4.442, 5.4733, 5.541–5.5423; see also 3.5, 4, 4.063, 4.431.

[2] F. H. Bradley: *The Principles of Logic*, Vol. I, Bk. I *passim*, for items quoted see p. 2; *Appearance and Reality*, Chs. xv, xxiv.

[3] B. Bosanquet: *Knowledge and Reality*, Chs. I–IV; *Logic*, Vol. I, Bk. I *passim*; *The Essentials of Logic*, Lects. II, IV–VIII.

[4] G. E. Moore: 'The Nature of Judgement'.

[5] G. Frege: *Begriffschrift*, Sect. 2 (G & B, pp. 1–2); 'Function and Concept' (G & B, p. 34); *Grundgesetze*, Vol. I, Sect. 5 (G & B, p. 156).

[6] See B. Russell: *The Principles of Mathematics*, on Moore's influence see pp. xviii, 24, 448n, on Frege's influence see Sect. 477.

[7] B. Russell: *Principia Mathematica*, 2nd ed., Vol. I, p. 43.

perception, considered as an actual occurrence, is a relation of four terms, namely $a$ and $b$ and $R$ and the percipient.

Wittgenstein disagreed with this, though not because he objected in principle to accounts of judgement; on the contrary, he thought he had a more accurate one. Since thoughts as much as propositions have to be pictures, the relation involved in a judgement is not one between a person and the constituents of the fact, as Russell would have, but rather a relation between a psychical fact and the fact that is being judged. Wittgenstein puts the argument in the formal mode. On Russell's theory the proposition '$A$ judges that $p$' would be relational, with $A$ and the constituents of $p$ as the relata, and Wittgenstein's objection is that this involves a misunderstanding of the content of the proposition. In saying '$A$ judges that $p$' one does not claim that $A$, as a *person*, stands in some relation to a *fact*. What one claims is that in $A$'s head there is a psychical fact with certain properties, the properties which any fact which pictures $p$ must have.

In fact, far from being opposed to theories of judgement, Wittgenstein was concerned to fill in their lacunae. He once wrote Russell:[1]

I can now express my objection to your theory of judgement exactly: I believe it is obvious that, from the proposition 'A judges that (say) $a$ is in a relation $R$ to $b$', if correctly analysed, the proposition '$aRb$ $\vee \sim aRb$' must follow directly *without the use of any other premiss.* This condition is not fulfilled by your theory.

The proviso that '$aRb$ or not $aRb$' must follow without further premises is another way of saying that one cannot judge nonsense. If $A$ can judge that $aRb$, then $aRb$ must be a possible state of affairs, i.e. either '$aRb$' or '$\sim aRb$' is true. Theories of judgement, if they are to be complete, must both recognize and explain the fact that not any combination of words can be a judgement. One does not judge, to use Wittgenstein's example in *Notes on Logic*, that 'this table penholders the book',[2] and one does not judge this not because it is never true but because such a collocation of words would never be admitted as a judgement. This is a good

---

[1] Letter 8: June, 1913.    [2] *NL* I 118–20; cf. 5.5422.

criticism, as Russell, to judge from Wittgenstein's next letter to him, must have quite adequately acknowledged:[1]

I am very sorry to hear [Wittgenstein wrote] that my objection to your theory of judgement paralyses you. I think it can only be removed by a correct theory of propositions.

This was a remedy that he called for again in the *Notes on Logic*:[2]

The epistemological questions concerning the nature of judgement and belief cannot be solved without a correct apprehension of the form of the proposition.

In the *Tractatus* we can see Wittgenstein following his own advice. He gives us first 'a correct theory of propositions', namely the picture theory of the 2.1's. True to his claim this theory of propositions fills the lacuna in the theory of judgement. Pictures are made up of constituents which have the same form as the objects for which they stand; therefore, a combination of these constituents is possible when and only when the corresponding combination is possible for the objects. Then, having filled the lacuna, he goes on in the 3.0's to draw the conclusion that it is impossible to judge nonsense—the conclusion that he had re-proached Russell for not being able to draw. He puts this in a number of different ways: what is judgeable is also possible;[3] a judgement already guarantees the possibility of the state of affairs which is judged;[4] and we cannot judge anything illogical, because this would require that we judge *illogically*.[5] The last remark looks paradoxical, but I take it to mean that to judge something illogical would require that we *act* in a way that it is not in our power to act, that we combine elements which, because of their forms, cannot be combined. An illogical judgement is an impossible entity, because it would be the result of an impossible activity.

These examples should be enough to show that the *Tractatus* belongs to the age of theories of judgement. Now, Wittgenstein's own theory comes in the 3.0's. Only Wittgenstein never uses the

---

[1] Letter 9: Hochreit, Post Hohenberg, Nieder-Österreich, 22.7.13.
[2] *NL* 1 155-7.      [3] 3.02.      [4] 3.02.      [5] 3.03's.

word 'judgement' ('Urteil'); his word is 'thought' ('Gedanke')
which he introduces at 3:

A logical picture of facts is a thought.

This is all the definition of 'thought' there is, and it is hardly
enough to forestall difficulties. For example, 3 seems to give us the
identity: logical picture = thought. 5.542, as I have said, suggests
the identity: thought = psychical fact. But both these equations
cannot be right, as the following argument shows. Since 2.182
says that every picture is a logical one, a picturing spatial fact is a
logical picture. On these two equations it must, then, be both a
thought and a psychical fact. But a spatial fact cannot be a psychical
fact. They are two different kinds of facts and cannot, at least
without some sort of qualification, be said to be the same. I want to
explain what Wittgenstein means by 'thought' by showing how
this particular confusion is to be straightened out. I shall take up
the three terms in the equations in order: first 'logical picture',
then 'thought', then 'psychical fact'.

## 1a. LOGICAL PICTURES

'Logical picture' is liable to be misunderstood. It is tempting,
for reasons I need not go into, to treat the concepts of 'logical
picture' ('logische Bild') and 'logical proto-picture' ('logische
Urbild') as the same. But it is also a mistake. Because a logical
proto-picture is not an ordinary picture of facts but a picture
variable; that is, it is what results from replacing the constants in a
picture with variables.[1] And to call something a logical picture is
to say no more than that it is a picture which has, either by nature
or by adoption, the form of the fact it pictures. Wittgenstein's
insisting that, say, a spatial picture is *at the same time* a logical
picture[2] means only that this picture, in addition to its form as a
(spatial) fact, *also* has the form of the (possibly non-spatial) fact it
pictures. When we say that something is a spatial picture, this
means that it is a picturing fact of the spatial form. In exactly
the same way, when we say that something is a logical picture,
this means that it is a picturing fact with the form of the fact it

[1] 3.315.        [2] 2.182.

pictures, with logical form. But note: a logical picture is a picture
in the ordinary sense, a particular complex of picturing elements.

What is the criterion of identity of a logical picture? It will be
extremely useful later to be clear on this. To start, what are the
identity criteria of *facts* and *sense*? A fact is a configuration of
objects. It is clear that when the objects are different, the facts
must be different; and from Wittgenstein's insistence on a fact's
being a *definite* combination of objects,[1] it is also clear that when
the objects are the same but the configuration different, the facts
are different. Now, *sense* is at the other end of the scale. The
sense of a picture is, by definition,[2] what the picture represents.
In general, then, if *A* and *B* are pictures of the same fact, then no
matter how different they are in their own right as facts, they have
the same sense. 'Sense', it seems, is Wittgenstein's word for what is
common to all pictures of the same subject. Now, what of logical
pictures? As we know, a picture is a fact. But does this mean that a
picture has the same criterion of identity as a fact? I think not.
Take first the case of propositional signs. A propositional sign is a
fact too,[3] but does it therefore have the same criterion of identity
as a fact? A propositional sign is composed of simpler signs, and on
these Wittgenstein is helpful. The simplest sign of all, viz. a name,
stands for an object, Wittgenstein says; and he adds:[4]

'*A*' is the same sign as '*A*'.

the best explanation of which is the ampler version in *Notes on
Logic*:[5]

It is to be remembered that names are not things but classes: 'A' is the
same letter as 'A'.

The identity criterion of a sign is not the same as that of an
object, though a sign is an object. Is it, then, that since a sign is
not only an object but an object that stands for something, signs
are the *same* sign when they stand for the *same* object? This, we see
later in the *Tractatus*, is not what Wittgenstein had in mind. By a
sign he means a class, but the class, as we see in his distinction
between signs and symbols, is defined by physical similarity

---

[1] 2.031, 2.14, 3.14, 3.141, 3.1431, 3.1432.
[2] 2.221.     [3] 3.14b.     [4] 3.203.     [5] *NL* v 29–30.

alone. Two different symbols can have the same sign (e.g. the sign '*A*' can be used to refer to both *a* and *b*), but the sign is merely what is perceptible, and this is a matter of convention; we might, to avoid confusion, choose two different signs (e.g. use sign '*A*' for *a* and sign '*B*' for *b*).[1] Thus, physical similarity is the only condition for similarity of sign. '*A*' and '*B*' are always different signs, even if they stand for the same object; '*A*' and '*A*' are the same sign, even if they stand for different objects. From this I think one can generalize to signs of any sort and say that they too are the same when they are physically the same. '*aRb*' is the same propositional sign as '*aRb*' whether or not it has the same sense. Now, to bring the discussion back to pictures requires an additional step, because 'picture' is not just the genus of which 'propositional sign' is one species. Because, according to the way Wittgenstein uses the word, a picture always has a sense; a picture is a fact[2] when that fact is being used to express something.[3] Thus, a picture is more than just a sign, but it is at any rate a sign; and it is more than just a sense, but it does at any rate have a sense. If the parallel between propositions and pictures counts for anything, a picture is a sense as expressed by a particular sign. Its criterion of identity, then, must be the product of the identity criteria of both the sign which is the picture and the picture's sense. Then, finally, since a logical picture is a picture, its identity criterion must be the same: we have the same logical picture when we have physically similar signs saying the same thing.

1b. THOUGHTS

I am trying ultimately to explain 3, so I shall not make use of it here. Consider instead 3.5:

A propositional sign, applied and thought out, is a thought.

This cannot be taken as a definition of thought, because since the domain of thought is coextensive with the domain of pictures, the two terms in 3.5, 'thought' and 'propositional sign', are on different levels of generality. 3.5 is restricted to the domain of propositions, though not the less informative for that. It says that when

---

[1] 3.32–3.325.    [2] 2.141.    [3] 2.12, 2.202, 2.21, 2.22, 2.221.

we have a propositional sign applied, i.e. actually used, then we have a thought. That is, limiting attention to propositions, a thought is a propositional sign in use.

What happens when a propositional sign is used? Well, obviously part of what is involved is that there are names correlated with particular objects and there is a rule that such-and-such an arrangement of the names will say that the objects are arranged in such-and-such a way. This much the picture theory tells us. But there is another important step, and it is this step, I think, that Wittgenstein goes on in the 3.0's, in his theory of judgement, to take. There must be names with meaning and configurations with sense, but before one has a proposition there must also be a particular person on a given occasion putting certain of these names into one of the configurations, thereby making a judgement. The picture theory deals only with the preconditions for the use of any propositional sign, and what we are interested in now are the conditions for a single propositional sign's actually being used. So now we must turn to the judging mind; we must bring in *thinking* and *thought*. This is what 3.5 does. It says that when a propositional sign is applied to some situation, when a person actually assembles its elements to make an assertion, we have a thought out propositional sign. That is, in regard to propositions, thinking means the same as using a propositional sign. So, thinking must be the act of putting the elements together in a way that expresses something. Thus, a thought must be the elements as put together, i.e. not just a propositional sign but a propositional sign when it is the outcome of this act.

Explaining thought this way has some curious consequences, but that this is, none the less, what Wittgenstein is claiming seems to me confirmed by 3.11b:

The method of projection is to think out the sense of the proposition.

The way in which we project the fact into the proposition is the same as the thinking we do in framing the proposition. That is, in the case of propositions at least, the thinking is the projecting. This would also seem to confirm that a thought is the outcome of this act. If this is what thinking is, then a thought must be what projecting results in, i.e. a projection. But it is a projection not simply in the sense of a propositional sign, because projecting results not in a propositional sign but in a propositional sign with a sense. A thought, then, is a propositional-sign-plus-its-sense. Now, one curious consequence of this definition is that there can be no such thing as an unexpressed thought. A number of times Wittgenstein refers to the 'expression' of thoughts.[1] This way of speaking might be taken to suggest the ordinary view that thoughts are independent of the various ways of expressing them, that a thought can exist on its own and one can choose the way one wishes to express it: in written words, in spoken words, in non-verbal pictures, &c. But *if the expressions of thoughts are these various kinds of pictures* (and I take this to be proper elucidation of 'expressed') then, according to 3.11b, there can only be expressed thoughts. Thinking a sense is a method of projection; so it is impossible to think a sense except *in* or *through* some method of projection. If we are to think at all, we must put together elements in accordance with some method of projection or other. Thinking is not separable from this activity, and a thought is not separate from the results of this activity. But can the connexion between thinking and projecting be quite so close? Recall 3.5: an applied propositional sign is a thought. So, in this context at any rate, a thought is not something separate from and subsequently expressed in a propositional sign; it *is* a propositional sign. It is just the sign under certain conditions, namely when it is the outcome of a piece of projection, i.e. when it has sense. A second consequence of this definition is the identity criterion of a thought it gives us. A thought is a propositional-sign-plus-sense. So, its identity criterion is a double one: it includes the criteria of identity of both a sign and a sense. Thus, should I say to one person '*aRb*' and later to another '*aRb*', or even should a third person say '*aRb*', (where these all have the same sense), these are the same thought. Should I say '*aRb*' on one occasion and on another '*cSd*' (which means the same as '*aRb*'), these are different thoughts. Should I say '*aRb*' on one occasion and on another '*aRb*' (where this second now has a different sense), these too are

[1] See 3.1, 3.12, 3.2, 6.21; see also p. 3.

IWLA

different thoughts. This may be why in 3.11b Wittgenstein says that thinking is the *method* of projection. If a thought is what thinking results in, then thoughts will differ when the method of projection differs; and difference in method of projection always accompanies (because it is the cause of) difference in the physical appearance of the propositional sign. So, thoughts are the same when they are the same kind of projection of the same fact.

Now, one last step remains with thoughts: to generalize from propositions to pictures, which, so far as I can see, is easily enough done. Projecting is something that occurs with all pictures, not just propositional signs. Thus, if in the case of propositional signs thinking is projecting, then it must be for pictures in general that thinking is projecting. Thus, too, if a thought is the propositional-sign-plus-sense in the one case, it must in general be a picturing-fact-plus-sense.

## IC. PSYCHICAL FACTS

I think psychical facts become clear once we settle the relation between logical pictures and thoughts. 3 says that a thought is a picture, any kind of fact so long as it satisfies the conditions of being a picture; (this is what I take the force of 'logical picture' to be). Since it is impossible for a picture not to have a sense, 3 in the end amounts to another formulation of the conclusion I reached above about thought: a thought is a picturing-fact-plus-sense. The equation thoughts = logical pictures is right, after all; and not by accident are the criteria of identity of thoughts and of logical pictures the same.

But now we can see why the equation thoughts = psychical facts was a mistake. Since a thought ('Gedanke') is a picturing-fact-plus-sense, and since a psychical fact is only *one* kind of picturing fact, it is only one kind of thought. One could put it like this. There are in the *Tractatus* both thoughts-1, which are expressed in pictures of all kinds (propositions, diagrams, &c.) —this is the primary sense of thought—and thoughts-2, psychical facts. Thoughts-1 are always expressed in a picture of some kind, even if that picture be of the private kind like thoughts-2. Thoughts-1 are the 'Gedanken' of the *Tractatus*. Thoughts-2 are never even named in the *Tractatus*, and I hope I do not confuse things by calling them thoughts. (Perhaps I might repeat: in the *Tractatus*, whenever the word 'thought' ('Gedanke') appears it means thought-1). Thoughts-2, though, certainly do enter Wittgenstein's ideas,[1] and my aim in contrasting thoughts-1 with thoughts-2 has been to show just how wide a concept 'Gedanke' is in the *Tractatus*.

Wittgenstein's theory of judgement says that judging is putting objects which stand for other objects into patterns which form pictures. This is not exactly a lot to say about judgement. But Wittgenstein would answer that there are reasons why, no matter what the temptations, one should not say more. He particularly thinks one should not say more about the nature of the elements that appear in pictures (apart from their having the one characteristic that they can stand for objects). In this regard he is the spiritual heir of Moore to some extent, but of Bradley even more. It was one of Bradley's great insights that philosophers might not have to answer half the questions they customarily asked themselves about images, impressions, &c., or rather that half the questions they asked were just not philosophical. Moore agreed with Bradley on this but thought that Bradley had not yet gone far enough, and Wittgenstein, in his turn, thought that even Moore had not seen how far one had to go. The descent of this idea from Bradley to Wittgenstein is an interesting story, and worth a brief recounting for the light it throws on the question of how Wittgenstein thought epistemology connected with his subject.

Bradley thought that we should distinguish ideas considered as 'phenomena' from 'the way in which logic uses ideas';[2] ideas as phenomena may be worth studying in some field or other, but logic has its own way of using ideas and these alone need be studied by logic. By 'idea', Bradley tells us, he means 'a psychical fact',[3] and how logic uses a psychical fact he explains in this way. I have, say, the idea of horse, and, considered as a psychical fact,

---

[1] In addition to the 5.54's (the analysis of statements of the sort '*A* thinks that *p*'), see Letter 18: Cassino, 19.8.19, paras. 2, 4.

[2] F. H. Bradley: *The Principles of Logic*, Ch. 1, Sect. 3.      [3] Loc. cit.

it exists in my mind, along with sensations, emotions, and feelings, 'unique, the same with no other, nor yet with itself, but alone in the world of its fleeting moment'.[1] The content of my idea of horse can be given in a list of attributes; the horse I am imagining is, let us say, white, slender, standing, head bent to ground, &c. Now, when I make a judgement that a certain thing is a horse, I obviously do not mean that it has all the attributes that my image has. In order to avoid this absurdity, we must, Bradley thinks, separate an idea as psychical fact from an idea as symbol; and the idea as symbol is only a part of the idea as fact. What we do to make it a symbol is to 'cut off' that part of the content of our image which is not sufficiently universal: we cut off the particular colour, the particular posture, &c., of the horse in our image, and what is left is 'fixed by the mind, and considered apart from the existence of the sign'; it is the 'meaning'.[2] '. . . this fragmentary part of the psychical event is all that in logic we know of or care for'.[3] But is a psychical event, fragmentary or otherwise, what we care for in logic? Moore, in his 1899 article, thought not.[4] Though Bradley separates the meaning, i.e. the symbol, from the idea, he still has not made the break sharp enough. Meaning, though no longer an idea, becomes instead an abstraction from an idea.[5] This half-way position, Moore argues, lands Bradley in a familiar infinite regress. On Bradley's account, we make a judgement by combining meanings, and we get our meanings for a particular judgement by using ideas with the essential cut off from the inessential and fixed by the mind. But to be able to do this cutting off means that we can already pick out an idea of a horse. So, before we make one judgement, we make a prior judgement about the character of our idea. But in order to make a judgement as to the character of this primary idea we must already have cut off the essential content from a secondary idea of horse, and so on, *ad infinitum*.[6] From this Moore concludes that meanings (or, as he prefers to call them, concepts) are completely distinct from ideas; there is no process of derivation of concepts from ideas which we,

---

[1] Op. cit., Ch. 1, Sect. 6.       [2] Op. cit., Ch. 1, Sect. 4.
[3] Op. cit., Ch. 1, Sect. 6.       [4] G. E. Moore: 'The Nature of Judgement'.
[5] Op. cit., p. 177.               [6] Op. cit., p. 178.

as judging agents, must perform. Concepts are a *genus per se,* irreducible to anything else; they are 'possible objects of thought', 'incapable of change', which 'may come into a relation with a thinker', though 'it is indifferent to their nature whether anybody thinks them or not'.[1]

This is now not far from Wittgenstein, though Wittgenstein goes further. He certainly agrees with Moore's argument; this is the point of his repeated warnings to philosophers that:[2]

Psychology is no more closely related to philosophy than any other natural science. . . .

Does not my study of sign-language correspond to the study of thought-processes, which philosophers used to consider so essential to the philosophy of logic? Only in most cases they got entangled in unessential psychological investigations, and with my method too there is an analogous risk.

But Wittgenstein does not say anything about a thinking mind's coming into relation with concepts, nor about any of the other things Moore claims for concepts. He does not use the word 'concept', nor any comparable word. He speaks of the 'elements' of pictures, of 'names', of 'simple signs'. The study of thought-processes is to be entirely replaced by the study of sign-language, and, strictly speaking, even Moore's kind of concept-talk goes beyond this. The study of thought-processes can be replaced by the single assertion that a thought is a picture. This is adequate even when the thought is private; this case is no different from any other; there is a fact (here a psychical one—but even this need not be said; in fact, the phrase is mine, not Wittgenstein's) which functions as and has all the necessary features of a picture. This may seem little to say, but to say more would lead us in one of two directions. If we are interested in these psychical facts, as many philosophers have been, then we can only say more by, for example, relating these facts to parts of our psychical life, and this, though a perfectly legitimate study, is an empirical one. Or if we are more interested in other kinds of picturing facts, such as propositional signs, we can only lapse into descriptions not of what

[1] Op. cit., pp. 178–9.
[2] 4.11121a, c; cf. *Nbk.* 10.11.14b; see also Letter 18: Cassino 19.8.19, paras. 2, 4.

must be the case in any language but of what is the case in a particular language. We can only say more, that is, by leaving philosophy.

I shall come back to this extreme purism of Wittgenstein's later; more has to be said about it. It was what caused Wittgenstein never to bother looking for examples of objects or of elementary propositions—except in the privacy of the *Notebooks*, and then hardly in a serious way; it made him scorn asking whether naming could possibly have the priority that his *a priori* arguments assigned to it, or whether analysis could possibly proceed as his *a priori* arguments required. And when he finally asked himself these questions, he decided that the answers upset the foundations of all theories of logical atomism.

### 2. *Wittgenstein's Criticism of Frege*

Wittgenstein's remarks about thoughts are only appreciated after one sees how much he extracts from them later in the *Tractatus*. The most interesting extraction is his criticism of Frege's assertion sign, i.e. judgement stroke ('Urteilstrich').[1] I have remarked before that Wittgenstein never speaks of judgement but only of thought. Frege, however, uses both words:[2]

. . . we need a special sign to assert that something or other is true. For this purpose I write the sign '⊢' before the name of the truth-value, so that in '⊢$2^2 = 4$' it is asserted that the square of 2 is 4. I make a distinction between *judgement* and *thought*, and understand by judgement the acknowledgement of the truth of a thought.

Now, Wittgenstein's use of 'thought' is quite different. In fact, since Wittgenstein must have been well acquainted with Frege's use,[3] perhaps he would be willing to have his theory of judgement summed up like this: Wittgenstein holds that, *pace* Frege, a *Gedanke* is an *Urteil*, that no distinction should be made, and that the second term is otiose.

Frege introduces the assertion sign in order to account for

---

[1] See 4.442; see also 3.143, 4.063, 4.064, 4.0641, 4.431, 5.02c; for other criticisms of Frege but not specifically of his theory of judgement see 3.325b, 4.1272h, 4.1273a, 5.132d, 5.4, 5.42b, 5.4733a, 5.521b, 6.1271, 6.232.

[2] Frege: *Grundgesetze der Arithmetik*, Vol. I, Sect. 5, (G & B, p. 156).

[3] See *NL* I 103–6, where Wittgenstein accepts Frege's argument.

suppositions. He argues that the only way to account for them is to draw a distinction between the content of a proposition and what we do with it: assert it, suppose it, &c.[1] A thought, then, is this unasserted content, 'a mere complex of ideas', something which produces in us only the idea of a state of affairs. Thus, judgements, as we have them in normal declarative sentences, are composed of two parts: the content and something which asserts either that the content is true or that it is false. (Perhaps the attribution to Frege of the extreme view that 'is true' or 'is false' is the real verb in any judgement, which Wittgenstein makes at 4.063c, does not do full justice to the subtlety of his position. But I shall leave this aside, since it is really only the Frege who appears in the *Tractatus* who need concern us.) Now, there is just enough truism in this doctrine (whether or not it is in all respects Frege's) to make it seem both attractive and reasonable; so, we must notice at exactly which point Wittgenstein directs his criticism. He begins with the idea that a declarative sentence has two parts: a content and the assertion of it. Certainly such a sentence makes an assertion; as Wittgenstein says, every proposition both *shows* how things stand and *says* that they do so stand.[2] But they certainly do not assert what Frege says they assert. No proposition can possibly assert of itself that it is true.[3] The propositon '*a* is to the left of *b*' asserts something, but something about *a* and *b* and their spatial relation; it does not make an assertion about the truth or falsity of anything, let alone whether it is true or false that *a* is to the left of *b*. To make this assertion, one would need a second proposition. This is a good point. And Wittgenstein may be right that, when Frege splits propositions into content and assertion sign, he puts himself in a position where he has to say that the assertion in a proposition is something or other, however it should be expressed, about the content of the proposition. But the assertion is, clearly, nothing about the content; the assertion is already contained in the content, and this is why an assertion sign, Wittgenstein says, is logically altogether meaningless and is no more a part of a proposition than would be, say, the number we assigned it. So, we can distinguish

---

[1] Frege: 'Function and Concept', (G & B, p. 34).    [2] 4.022b.
[3] 4.442; see also 4.064, 4.0641.

in Wittgenstein's attack on Frege two elements: the negative contention that Frege's theory lands him in an untenable position concerning what a proposition asserts, and the positive contention that the assertion in a proposition is already contained in the content. The positive contention is an elaboration of Wittgenstein's own theory of judgement. What does the asserting in the proposition '*a* is to the left of *b*' is that we have put the names '*a*' and '*b*' in a configuration which expresses something. Arrangements of elements are the way we do in fact and the only way we can express something about arrangements of objects. This is why at one place Wittgenstein accuses Frege of thinking of a proposition (to be more accurate he should have said *Gedanke*) as a complex kind of name.[1] For both Frege and Wittgenstein a *Gedanke* singles out a particular state of affairs. But a *Gedanke* for Frege *indicates* a state of affairs, refers to it but says nothing about it. And it is because Frege thinks of *Gedanken* as complex names that he is led to introduce the assertion sign. In contrast, Wittgenstein thinks that giving names a significant configuration produces something generically different from a name, a fact. So, what I am calling Wittgenstein's positive contention comes down really to two points: (i) the only way to single out a state of affairs is with a fact (if Frege wants to maintain that his *Gedanken* single out states of affairs, then he must allow that they are facts), and (ii) it is that a proposition is a fact that makes it an assertion (there is no ground for Frege's distinction between a *Gedanke* and an assertion). Fail to see that a thought is a fact, Wittgenstein thinks, and you are led to the introduction of both a useless piece of logical equipment, the assertion sign, and an unnecessary concept, the *judgement*.

[1] See 3.143c; see also 5.02c.

# X

# SENTENCES

## 1. *Wittgenstein's Theory of Symbolism*

UNTIL now I have followed the general practice of translating 'Satz' as 'proposition'. This has been the usual translation in large part because it has also been the usual interpretation. Beginning with Ramsey in his review of the *Tractatus*,[1] interpreters have assumed that when Wittgenstein uses 'Satz' he means what philosophers have traditionally meant by 'proposition'. I want to put this in question now, so for a while I shall use 'Satz' untranslated.

*Sätze* are one kind of thought. They are thoughts the expressions of which we perceive through the senses,[2] where the elements are words,[3] either spoken or written.[4] *Sätze* are the class of thoughts that interests Wittgenstein most, and to explain them he introduces this elaboration of the picture metaphor. *Sätze* are pictures, but they are, more precisely, pictures which we produce by projecting facts into other facts through mechanisms which can, though they need not, distort the original considerably.[5] What Wittgenstein had in mind in speaking of projections ('Projektionen') comes out in his other writings, where he was always more willing to use examples.[6] He had in mind, evidently, geometrical projections, because he asks us in his 'Logical Form' article to imagine:[7]

. . . two parallel planes, I and II. On plane I figures are drawn, say, ellipses and rectangles of different sizes and shapes, and it is our task to produce images of these figures on plane II. Then we can imagine two ways, amongst others, of doing this. We can, first, lay down a law of projection—say that of orthogonal projection or any other—and then proceed to project all figures from I into II, according to this law. Or, secondly, we could proceed thus: We lay down the rule that every ellipse

[1] F. P. Ramsey: Critical Notice of the *Tractatus*, repr. *The Foundations of Mathematics*, see esp. p. 274.
[2] 3.1, 3.11a.   [3] 3.14, 3.141.   [4] 3.11, 3.321.   [5] 3.11 *et seq.*
[6] See *Nbk.* 15.11.14a; *LF* pp. 164, 166; *Bl. Bk.* p. 37 (also p. 33: 'process of projection'); Moore: 'Wittgenstein's Lectures in 1930–33' in *Philosophical Papers*, pp. 263 *et seq.*; cf. 4.0141
[7] *LF* p. 164.

on plane I is to appear as a circle in plane II, and every rectangle as a
square in II. Such a way of representation may be convenient for us if
for some reason we prefer to draw only circles and squares on plane II.
Of course, from these images the exact shapes of the original figures on
plane I cannot be immediately inferred. We can only gather from them
that the original was an ellipse or a rectangle. In order to get in a single
instance at the determinate shape of the original we would have to know
the individual method by which, e.g., a particular ellipse is projected
into the circle before me. The case of ordinary language is quite
analogous. If the facts of reality are the ellipses and rectangles on plane I,
the subject-predicate and relational forms correspond to the circles and
squares in plane II. These forms are the norms of our particular
language into which we project in *ever so many different* ways *ever so
many different* logical forms.

Perhaps the easiest way to think of this is in terms of a particular
class of geometrical projections, maps. A *Satz* is a map of a certain
territory, and we get different maps of the same teritory by varying
the projection. In fact, maps can deviate so grossly from the
territory they map that we may sometimes wonder whether they
are maps at all,[1] but we see that they are when we understand the
method of projection.

Now, Wittgenstein uses this elaboration of the picture metaphor
to draw the following distinction. In the 2's he spoke simply of
pictures. But when in the 3's he takes up *Sätze*, he has a three-
fold distinction: he speaks at various times of the 'Satzzeichen'
(in both the Ogden and the Pears and McGuinness translations:
'propositional sign'), the 'Satz' (both in Ogden and in Pears and
McGuinness: 'proposition'), and the 'sinnvoller Satz' (in Ogden:
'significant proposition', in Pears and McGuinness: 'proposition
with a sense'). I want to explain a simpler distinction first and
return to this one later. I have already explained what 'sign' means;
its correlate notion, 'symbol', is introduced like this: a sign is what
can be perceived of a symbol.[2] From this, we get the impression
that a symbol is more than *but none the less includes* a sign,[3]
and this impression is confirmed, I think, by later propositions in
the *Tractatus*. For example, Wittgenstein speaks of what is

[1] Cf. 4.011.          [2] 3.32; cf. 3.1.
[3] This point and the references in the following note were brought to my
attention by McGuinness and Pears in their class.

essential in different symbols that can serve the same purpose.[1] Presumably, in this context serving the same purpose means having the same sense. So, since *different* symbols have the *same* sense, symbols must differ by having different signs. The sign must, therefore, be an essential part of the symbol, and symbols will be signs-plus-sense. So, we come again on this familiar formula, only here in the sign-symbol distinction we have finally met the genus whose species we were meeting in the distinctions in the last chapter. Picturing facts are signs; both pictures (picturing-facts-plus-sense) and thoughts (which are also picturing-facts-plus-sense) are symbols.

Now to apply this distinction to the three-fold one of *Satzzeichen*, *Satz*, and *sinnvoller Satz*. *Satzzeichen* are, obviously, signs; and *sinnvolle Sätze* must be *Satzzeichen*-plus-sense and so must be symbols. Where does this leave *Sätze*? That they are more than signs their definition says,[2] but that they are not symbols is made clear by 3.13c, which says that a *Satz* does not actually contain its sense, but only the possibility of expressing it. A *Satz*, then, is somewhere between sign and symbol. It is, to return to its definition, the *Satzzeichen* plus its projective relation to the world. How much of the whole projection this includes can be explained as follows. A whole projection may be diagrammed like this:

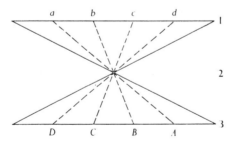

A projection includes objects, e.g. *a*, *b*, *c*, and *d*, configured in a certain way to form a fact (level 1); it includes a method of projection, i.e. a translation device—here the device is one of reversal of order (level 2); it includes names, e.g. *A*, *B*, *C*, *D*, which in configuration form a *Satzzeichen* (level 3). Now how much of this

---

[1] 3.341b, 3.3411, 3.344.          [2] 3.12.

a *Satz* includes is explained in the long proposition at 3.13. A *Satzzeichen* is level 3 simply. A *Satz*, however, is everything in this diagram except what is projected,[1] i.e. everything but level 1. Actually, though, if a *Satz* excludes level 1, then certain subtractions must be made from level 3. If we do not know that the objects are *a*, *b*, *c*, and *d*, then we cannot have the real names *A*, *B*, *C*, *D* on level 3. All we can have are variables, or more accurately names without bearers, dummy names. A *Satz*, then, may be diagrammed:

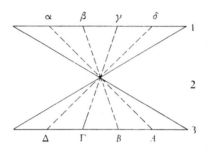

But since on level 3 a *Satz* does include the form of the dummy names, and since it does include level 2, i.e. the method of projection, in a sense it does include level 1, i.e. what is projected. It does not include what is projected itself, but it does include the form of what is projected, i.e. its possibility.[2] This now explains why, on this account of *Satz*, a *Satz* does not include a sense. To have a sense one must have names and not just dummy names; one must know what objects are arranged in this way. So, again, a *Satz* includes not any particular sense but only the possibility of expressing a number of different senses.[3] Or, another way of putting this, the *Satz* will contain only the form of its sense and not its content.[4]

A *Satz*, therefore, is far from what Ramsey thought. It is not that which is common to different expressions of the same sense. A *Satz* itself does not even have a sense; it can, indeed, express different senses. A *Satz* is only a *Satzzeichen* plus the skeleton of the relations which this sign can have to a class of facts. That is, it is a combination of words along with their syntactical application.

[1] 3.13a.        [2] 3.13b.        [3] 3.13c.        [4] 3.13e.

For example, 'John loves Mary'—as it stands here on this page, apart from the context of a particular occasion of its use—is a *Satz*. We do not know what objects the names 'John' and 'Mary' are correlated with, and so we do not know its sense; still we do know that 'John' and 'Mary' are names and that they can be correlated with only one kind of thing. This brings us to *sinnvoller Satz*. The *sinnvoller Satz* is a *Satz* on a particular occasion of its use, a *Satz* when its names are used referringly. This is why at 4 Wittgenstein defines *sinnvoller Satz* as a thought; we have just been told at 3.5 that a thought is a *Satzzeichen* when it is in *use*.

The best way to think of 'Satz' is as 'sentence'. But perhaps if 'proposition' will not do for 'Satz', it might do for 'sinnvoller Satz'. This is closer, yet still not on the mark. Suppose one person says 'the cat is on the mat' and another says 'Die Katze ist auf der Matte'. As we are taught from the start of our philosophical careers, these are the same proposition, but, as we have seen, they are clearly not the same *sinnvoller Satz*. The best way to think of 'sinvoller Satz' is as 'significant sentence' or—a fuller version—as 'sentence plus its sense'. If one wants a comparison from outside the *Tractatus* for these terms of Wittgenstein's, it would be best to forget 'proposition' altogether and to look to more recent philosophical discussion. Strawson, in 'On Referring', distinguishes a sentence from the use of a sentence,[1] and this is precisely, I should say, Wittgenstein's distinction between a sentence and a significant sentence. Also Wittgenstein makes with his distinction some of the same points Strawson makes with his. Strawson says that it is not sentences that are true or false but sentences used on particular occasions, sentences when their referring expressions successfully refer. Wittgenstein's point can be put in almost the same words: it is not sentences which are true or false but sentences when they are used, sentences when their names are co-ordinated with objects. There is an interesting divergence between Strawson and Wittgenstein over the word 'sense'. Strawson stresses that questions about sense have to do with sentences, and questions about truth and falsity with the use of sentences. The way Wittgenstein uses 'sense' is very different from this. For Wittgenstein the sense

[1] P. F. Strawson: 'On Referring', see esp. pp. 27–29.

of a sentence is the particular claim the sentence makes about the world. So Wittgenstein would make a point which is different from Strawson's, though possibly compatible with it; he would stress that both questions about truth and falsity and questions about sense concern only the use of sentences. This, it may be repeated, is why Wittgenstein says at 3.13c that a sentence does not have a sense but has only the possibility of expressing one.

One last comment on terminology. Wittgenstein does not always, particularly after the 3's, bother to mark the distinction between a *Satz* and a *sinnvoller Satz*; he simply uses 'Satz' and trusts to context to show when it should be read 'sinnvoller Satz'.[1] Though 'Satz' lends itself to this treatment as no one English word will, I shall do likewise with 'sentence'. This practice is less confusing, I find, than any alternative I have been able to think of.

So far I have been dealing with the general features of Wittgenstein's theory of symbolism: that a sentence is a projection, and that only the use of a sentence is true or false, or has sense. I want next to consider what Wittgenstein says in answer to the question: how do the elements of sentences have meaning? Take names, for instance. Part of what is involved in understanding a name is knowing its form, just as knowing an object requires knowing its possibilities of occurrence in states of affairs. But does this not involve us in a paradox? For (i) the meanings of names can be explained in elucidations, (ii) elucidations are sentences containing the names, i.e. contexts in which the names can appear, and (iii) elucidations can only be understood when the meanings of these signs are already known.[2] Hence, we understand names through elucidations, and elucidations only if we understand names. Wittgenstein mentions but does not try to resolve the paradox, and one can perhaps see why. The paradox must be only apparent, since we do in fact learn the meanings of names. But *how* the paradox is evaded, *how* in fact we do learn names, is, Wittgenstein may consider, an empirical matter. But he has brought the paradox up; if not to resolve it, then why? I think what interests him about it is made the subject of the 3.31's. Knowledge of the forms of sentence elements, no matter how achieved, is a necessary part of under-

---

[1] As it obviously should, e.g., at 4.01, 4.011, 4.021–4.024, &c.    [2] 3.263.

standing their meaning. Sentences, as Wittgenstein says at 3.3, are the basic carriers of sense, and not only names but any part of a sentence that helps characterize its sense has meaning only in the context of a sentence.[1] The first claim, about sentences, is true by the definition of sense.[2] The second, I think, is the same as the claim he makes at one point in the pre-*Tractatus* writings. In Chapter II.3 I cited Frege's argument that concepts must be completely defined and Wittgenstein's parallel argument that signs, either names or forms, have to be completely introduced in a symbolism. This is what the argument of the 3.31's comes down to; the conclusion is to be found in either 3.311 or 3.314:

An expression presupposes the forms of all sentences in which it can occur. . . . An expression has meaning only in a sentence.

Wittgenstein's pre-*Tractatus* thesis about the complete introduction of indefinables applied to both names and forms. I think the term 'expression' ('Ausdruck'), which runs through the 3.31's, also covers both names and functions; there are several considerations pro and con, but conclusive, I think, is Wittgenstein's equation of 'expression' and 'symbol' at 3.31a. Expressions must include functions, because symbols do.[3] If I am right, then we get an expression by, for example, dropping out the '$a$' in '$aRb$'; I shall write this expression as '( )$Rb$'. Now, Wittgenstein uses the word 'variable' in two senses in the 3.31's. The '( )' in '( )$Rb$' is a variable;[4] in fact, the way we see what expressions a sentence contains is by substituting variables in this sense for its constant elements. Then, Wittgenstein also calls the whole symbol '( )$Rb$' a variable; it is a sentence variable;[5] that is, it can take on different values all of which will be sentences. In the pre-*Tractatus* writings his point was, to put it in this *Tractatus* vocabulary, that any sentence variable, i.e. any expression, could be understood only when we have understood all of its possible occurrences in a symbolism—its form. And here the only difference in the point Wittgenstein is making is, I think, that he puts it still more generally. It is true not just of a variable in the second sense, i.e.

[1] See 3.3, 3.31; cf. Frege: *Grundlagen*, p. x, Sects. 60, 62, 106; also *PI* para. 49; I owe the references to Frege and *PI* to M. Dummett: 'Nominalism'.
[2] See 2.221.     [3] See 3.323.     [4] See 3.312b, 3.314a–b, 3.315.     [5] See 3.313.

an expression, but of a variable in either sense that it has meaning only in the context of a sentence—only when we recognize its form. It is essential even to variables in the first sense that they can be conceived of as sentence variables.[1] A variable has a form, which specifies the position in the sentence it can occupy; even the variable name carries along with it the specification of the sentences it will fit.[2]

Though it is a familiar point I want to follow out what Wittgenstein says about variables a little further, because it is soon to figure in his criticism of ordinary language and his recommendation of ideal notations. Suppose we take the sentence '$\phi a$' and change one of its constituents to a variable, getting the proto-picture '$\phi(\ )$'. But suppose we go on to replace the remaining constant with a variable; we then get the logical proto-picture '$[\ ](\ )$'.[3] I have been using brackets for my variables. But variables appear in definite positions in sentences and so have definite forms; a variable's form, one might say, is not variable. To indicate this I have used different kinds of brackets: I have used '$(\ )$' for signs like the '$a$' in '$\phi a$', '$[\ ]$' for signs like '$\phi$' in '$\phi a$'; and to complete my variable language I shall use '$\{\ \}$' for signs like '$R$' in '$aRb$'. Such a language shows that a variable is a sign which specifies the form of what can be substituted for it; in this sense a variable *is* a form. This is why Wittgenstein equates the *stipulation of values* with a *variable*;[4] the stipulation of its values is the specification of what form they can have, and the variable in itself specifies the form. Thus, no matter how abstract a variable is, there is no indeterminateness in the range of its values.[5] This helps elucidate the claim that not only names and functions but also variables can be understood only in the context of a sentence. But Wittgenstein has another point to make. We stipulate the values of a variable without reference to the meaning of any symbol.[6] Take the two cases of an ordinary proto-picture and a logical proto-picture, '$(\ )Rb$' and '$(\ )\ \{\ \}\ (\ )$'. In '$(\ )Rb$' the range of its values is determined by stipulating that we can substitute in the variable place only signs of the $(\ )$-form. In the more abstract '$(\ )\ \{\ \}\ (\ )$' the range is determined by stipulat-

---

[1] See 3.314a.        [2] See 3.314b.        [3] See 3.315.
[4] 3.316b.            [5] 3.316a.            [6] 3.317c, d.

ing that we can substitute in the appropriate places only signs of the ( )- or { }-form. Note that in neither case need we bring in meanings in order to make the stipulation clear. This last is not an especially surprising remark, and we must now see why Wittgenstein chooses to stress it so much.

## 2. *Ideal* versus *Ordinary Language*

The *Tractatus*, without doubt, contains criticisms of ordinary language. There is this one, for example: A sign differs from a symbol in such a way that sameness of sign is no guarantee of sameness of symbol. The same sign can be used in different symbols.[1] Not only *can* this occur, it *does*. It occurs frequently in ordinary language, and many, perhaps most, philosophical problems are not problems at all but only confusions generated by such confusing features of ordinary language.[2]

It must have been criticisms like this that led Russell on the first page of his Introduction to the *Tractatus* to say:

In order to understand Mr Wittgenstein's book, it is necessary to realize what is the problem with which he is concerned. In the part of his theory which deals with Symbolism he is concerned with the conditions which would have to be fulfilled by a logically perfect language.

Wittgenstein's picture theory, Russell evidently would maintain, is not a theory of language in general; it is, rather, a description of the features of the logically perfect language. This reading of the *Tractatus* still has its adherents.[3] Yet, it is a lot to conclude from Wittgenstein's few criticisms of ordinary language. I think that it does not follow at all, and that once his criticisms are understood, it is clear he had something very different in mind.

With the aid of Wittgenstein's distinction between sign and symbol, one can catalogue at least some of the sorts of confusions ordinary language fosters. (i) Ordinary language can use the same sign in different symbols. It can do this in two ways. (ia) It can use the same sign to stand for objects of the same form, or, still more confusing, (ib) it can use the same sign to fill different types of roles in the symbolism. Also, (ii) it can use different signs in such a similar

---

[1] 3.321.      [2] 3.324, 4.002b–d, 4.003.
[3] See I. M. Copi: 'Objects, Properties, and Relations in the *Tractatus*', pp. 145–7.

KWLA

way in the symbolism that one is led to believe that they are the same type of symbol. Examples of (ia) would be simple ones like using 'John' to refer to more than one person, and Wittgenstein does not bother to pursue this kind of example in the *Tractatus*. Examples of (ii) are the sort discussed by Ryle in 'Systematically Misleading Expressions'. We use 'John' and 'the present King of France', i.e. different signs, in such a similar way in our sentences that it looks as if they are of the same form. We use them both as grammatical subjects, and this tempts us into believing that they are both names and have meaning only by standing for something, when actually, to use my brackets language, one is a ( )-word and the other is of the form [ ] ( ), i.e. it speaks of the ( ) which is [ ]. Or, again, we use 'exists' and 'is red', different signs, in such a grammatically similar way that we think they are both [ ]-words, whereas, on the contrary, the former indicates that the sentence in which it occurs is not of the [ ] ( )-form at all, but of the existentially quantified form.[1] Why Wittgenstein does not explore these examples in the *Tractatus* is less easy to see. For all of his examples are of (ib), cases where we use the same sign with different forms. For instance (and this is Wittgenstein's example), we use the same sign 'is' as copula, sign of identity, and verb of existence. Far from being the same 'idea' or 'concept' in these three cases they are in fact three totally different symbols: 'is' as copula is one part of [ ]-words, as sign of equality it is a { }-word, and as expression of existence it indicates the form of a sentence, '∃ . . .'. Or of the sentence (again Wittgenstein's example) 'Green is green', where the first word is a proper name and the last an adjective, it is not enough to say that it uses the same word with different meanings. One is a ( )-word and the other a [ ]-word. Philosophers continually fasten on to similarity in sign as if it were indicative of some similarity of importance, a presumption, as these examples show, with little to justify it.[2]

How can we avoid these errors?[3] Well, obviously, by impressing on people the ( )-ness or [ ]-ness or { }-ness of words. Wittgenstein has in mind a specific way of doing this; we can avoid these errors,

[1] See 5.52's.  [2] 3.324.

[3] My ideas in this paragraph were greatly helped by McGuinness' and Pears' discussion in their class; I do not know whether either agrees with my conclusions.

he says, by reforming our symbolism in such a way that the signs themselves will keep us aware of forms.[1] My brackets language is such a symbolism; in it difference of form in symbols is embodied in difference of shape in signs. Suppose we required that the words of ordinary language always be used with their brackets. Then, instead of 'is' and 'is' and 'is', we should have '(is . . .)' and '{is}' and '∃ . . .'. That we are dealing with symbols with different roles in language is now apparent. Hence, we will no longer apply the same sign in different symbols: the copula '(is . . .)' and the sign of identity '{is}' now have different appearances and so are different signs; Mr. Green's name and his properties are different signs because they are words of different styles. Also we can no longer apply different signs in the same way, because we have an infallible guide to difference in role in a symbolism in the difference in appearance of the signs.[2] Wittgenstein says that Frege's or Russell's logical symbolism meets his requirements, evidently, because, in each, lower-case roman letters are used for what I call ( )-words, upper-case for { }-words, and Greek letters for [ ]-words; also sentences which are quantified in form are of a different shape altogether from sentences of a non-quantified form: e.g. '$(\exists x)\phi x$' in contrast to '$\phi a$'.[3] No doubt, though, neither my brackets language nor Frege's and Russell's logical symbolism has carried this use of different style signs for different form symbols far enough to exclude all errors. But with sufficient reforms of this nature signs become such that mistakes are almost impossible. As Wittgenstein says:[4]

Now, too, we understand our feeling that once we have a sign-language in which everything is all right, we already have a correct logical point of view.

The idea of a logical syntax was not Wittgenstein's innovation. Russell's Theory of Types had already suggested that the grammatical form of a sentence may not be its real form,[5] and in this the notion of logical syntax is latent. That is to say, the Theory of Types does suggest that grammatical syntax permits combinations of words which, considered logically, are impermissible, and that

---

[1] 3.325a.          [2] 3.325a.          [3] 3.325b.
[4] 4.1213; cf. 6.122.          [5] See 4.0031; cf. 4.002d, *LF* p. 162.

what we need is a logical syntax, which will tell us which *types* can go with which. But two features of Wittgenstein's logical syntax should especially be noticed; one, no doubt, is also a feature of Russell's, the other definitely is not. The first is that logical syntax is the syntax of any language; it is not meant as the specification of the conditions which must be satisfied by an ideal language. We derive the rules of logical syntax, Wittgenstein says, from observing how signs signify,[1] from considering their use when they have sense.[2] The signs of ordinary language signify in a certain way and have significant uses; so they obey a logical syntax. The only difference in this respect between an ideal and ordinary language is that with the latter it is hard to see the logical syntax, with the former it is hard not to see it. The second feature is one I have already touched on, namely, that in setting up logical syntax the meaning of signs does not (and, Wittgenstein adds here, ought never to) play a role.[3] This definitely cannot be said for the Theory of Types,[4] with what consequences we saw in Chapter III. Russell defines his types by reference to what they mean. Such-and-such a sign is first-order because it stands for a thing, such-and-such is second-order because it stands for the property of a thing, &c. Mention of the meaning of signs ought not to be made because any such mention must violate the Theory of Types itself; words like 'thing', 'property', &c., are typically ambiguous. Furthermore, no such mention *need* be made. In ordinary language that signs are names, properties, &c., shows in their application; in an ideal language it shows in the shape of the signs themselves.

Then how would Wittgenstein handle a Theory of Types? The 3.33's are his demonstration. Taking my brackets language as an ideal language, we see that it can be set up by, first, explaining that ( )-words are words of the form of '*a*', '*b*', &c., and so on for the other bracketed words; and, second, by drawing up the rules of logical syntax. There are only three rules (quantified sentences aside for the moment), and they can be stated like this. (i) A [ ]-word must be followed by one and only one ( )-word; (ii) a { }-word must be both preceded and followed by one and only one ( )-word; (iii) a ( )-word must be used in conjunction with

[1] 3.334.    [2] 3.326; cf. *Nbk.* 23.10.14f; see also 3.327.    [3] 3.33.    [4] 3.331.

either a [ ]-word or a { }-word. From this we can determine all permissible sentence forms: i.e. '[ ] ( )' and '( ) { } ( )', and all impermissible ones: i.e. '( ) ( )', '{ } [ ]', '[ ] { } [ ]', . . . . Now the whole point of the Theory of Types, according to Wittgenstein, is that no proposition can say anything about itself.[1] This is already said in my brackets language. When we use a function of, say, the [ ]-form, then the form of its argument is specified. We know that [ ]-words must be followed by ( )-words.[2] So, of course, it cannot be followed by itself, that is, by a [ ] ( )-sign. If this is not clear in ordinary language, it is amply clear in this brackets language: anything of the form '[ ] [ ] ( )' is nonsense.[3] So, Russell's paradox vanishes. 'All Cretans are liars' is paradoxical only by including itself as argument, and all we need do is to show someone the rules of logical syntax to prevent him from making this move.[4] Thus, in six sentences (3.332–3.333) Wittgenstein claims to have reproduced the whole of the Theory of Types. I think a better case can be made for this than might at first seem. The Theory of Types consists, roughly, of a restriction and a theoretical account of why the restriction is necessary, that is, of the Vicious Circle Principle and the arguments for and description of the hierarchy of types. 3.333 tries to do everything the Vicious Circle Principle does. Then at the back of Wittgenstein's claims about logical syntax, as I have indicated, is the Doctrine of Showing, and if we allow this in as part of his argument, then we have his version of the hierarchy of types too.

Now to go back to where I began. Russell in his Introduction only stated a conclusion; I want to look briefly at the kind of argument that has been used to reach it. Copi,[5] in an article I have already cited, is concerned with certain criticisms of the *Tractatus* made by Daitz,[6] the general tenor of which is that Wittgenstein's picture theory does not fit ordinary sentences. This prompts Copi to ask whether the *Tractatus* ever intended to account for ordinary sentences. He weighs the passages pro[7] and con,[8] admits arguments

---

[1] 3.332; cf. *NL* VI 1–3, 20–21.          [2] 3.333a.          [3] 3.333b, c.
[4] 3.333d.          [5] Copi: op. cit., p. 145.
[6] E. Daitz: 'The Picture Theory of Meaning', see esp. p. 59.
[7] 5.5563.          [8] 3.143, 3.323–5, 4.002, 5.53, 5.531, 5.533–4, 6.122.

of weight can be made on either side, but finally decides that the weightier is the argument con:[1]

The tendency to reject ordinary language seems to me to predominate. Wittgenstein was concerned with the construction of 'an adequate notation'. . . .
   I understand Wittgenstein to be primarily concerned with specifications for an artificial symbolic language. . . .

I think Copi is certainly right in saying to Daitz: you cannot criticize Wittgenstein by showing that what he says does not hold of ordinary language; you cannot take an example from ordinary language (like Daitz's 'Sophia hates Amos') and show that what he says about elementary sentences does not hold or yields contradictions; you cannot, that is, effectively criticize Wittgenstein's statements about elementary sentences until you have determined what an elementary sentence is like. And an elementary sentence is a queerer thing than Daitz seems to realize. But it is certainly wrong to justify this criticism as Copi does. What should be said to Daitz is that Wittgenstein's elementary sentences are not to be found in ordinary language, so her procedure is wrong. But elementary sentences are not an artificial and logically perfect language either. An ideal language is ideal, for Wittgenstein, because it makes clear features which are obscure in ordinary language, but the features that are being made clear, one should note, are the features of ordinary language. The features, the essentials, are precisely what is common to both. Thus, an ideal language is ideal simply in the sense that in it ideally only a fool will make a mistake, whereas in ordinary language even a philosopher might make one. Furthermore, elementary sentences are what ordinary sentences can be analysed into; elementary sentences build up into the sentences of ordinary language. Therefore, the dispute is generally quite misconceived. When Wittgenstein talks about elementary sentences, he is neither describing ordinary language nor giving the specifications of the logically perfect language. He is giving the specifications of *elementary* sentences, sentences underlying languages in general and so underlying ordinary language.

[1] Copi: op. cit., pp. 146, 147.

# XI

# CONCLUSION

## 1. *Recapitulation*

IN my first chapter I said that I was going to attack one interpretation of the *Tractatus* and to replace it with another. The interpretation I would attack stemmed, I claimed, from our tendency in philosophy to assume that any programme of reduction must be some kind of epistemological reduction, a reduction to units of experience. The truth in Wittgenstein's case, I suggested, is quite different. Analysis in the *Tractatus* is little like the analysis Russell talks about in *Our Knowledge of the External World*, and elementary sentences are quite different from, say, Carnap's protocol sentences. I said too that in the *Tractatus* Wittgenstein is interested in the features which any report about the world, any statement in the natural sciences, had to have, and that he meant by 'reports about the world' something more akin to what a scientist would mean than to what an epistemologist would mean. Now, in this final chapter, I shall try to piece together what I think the evidence for these contentions is.

## 2. *How Much can be Known About Elementary Sentences?*

I can imagine that off and on in the course of the earlier chapters this quite serious doubt about my arguments may have arisen. Perhaps I say too much about elementary sentences. In arguing, for instance, that they are always relational, or that they seem not to concern sense-data, I may have missed an important fact about the *Tractatus*. Perhaps these are things Wittgenstein himself does not know and, moreover, thinks that, as a logician, he need not know. Norman Malcolm tells of the time he asked Wittgenstein:[1]

... whether, when he wrote the *Tractatus*, he had ever decided upon anything as an *example* of a 'simple object'. His reply was that at that time his thought had been that he was a *logician*; and that it was not his business, as a logician, to try to decide whether this thing or that was a simple thing or a complex thing, that being a purely *empirical* matter!

[1] N. Malcolm: *Ludwig Wittgenstein: A Memoir*, p. 86.

And Moore mentions that Wittgenstein made the same admission for elementary sentences.[1] But one should not think that all the evidence points in this one direction. Most of the examples I used in Chapter VI (e.g. the analysis of the watch into its simple components) come from the *Notebooks*. And in the *Tractatus* Wittgenstein says that space, time, and colour are forms of objects, so he knows at least some of the kinds of complexes there are, e.g. spatial complexes; so he can and does say that there are, e.g., spatial objects. Without doubt, there are *some* features of objects and of elementary sentences about which agnosticism is very much in order, but not about *all*. And agnosticism gives no comforts unless one knows its limits.

So to return to the question: how much can be known about elementary sentences? Wittgenstein spends a whole section, the 5.55's, answering the question. Between 5 and 5.5 Wittgenstein tries to show that every sentence is the result of the successive application of the operation $(-----T)$ $(\xi,....)$ to elementary sentences; he gives, in other words, the general form of sentences. But once he has given it, he has to face some obvious difficulties. For instance, can one on this thesis account for generality (a question he answers in the 5.52's) or identity (5.53's) or sentences like '*A* has the thought *p*' (5.54's)? And, lastly, if one can give the general form of sentences, can one *also* give the general form of elementary sentences (5.55's)? Wittgenstein's answer is that one cannot. That is, one cannot *a priori*, for the simple reason that elementary sentences consist of names, that names can be of different forms, that the form of an elementary sentence is determined by the form of its names, that one cannot know the form of a name unless one is acquainted with the object, and that acquaintance with objects is, obviously, *a posteriori*.[2] So, logicians should have nothing to say about the forms of elementary sentences, and certainly can give nothing so specific as examples of them. This is why once more Russell comes in for criticism.[3] At the time of the *Tractatus* Russell was announcing again and again that one of logic's tasks was to

[1] G. E. Moore: 'Wittgenstein's Lectures in 1930–33', repr. *Philosophical Papers*, p. 296. For further evidence see *Nbk.* 23.5.15i; Letter 18: Cassino, 19.8.19, para. 4; *LF* pp. 163–4, 171.
[2] 5.55.          [3] 5.553a.

provide an 'inventory' or 'enumeration' of the kinds of atomic propositions there were. To this Wittgenstein quite rightly replies that if Russell thinks that logic can give inventories of atomic propositions, logic for Russell is not a strictly *a priori* study. The inventories Russell gave were hierarchies of atomic propositions: dyadic relations, triadic relations, tetradic relations, &c.[1] Wittgenstein's point is: how can Russell know this? Obviously only by experience. Take the rather extreme case of a 27-termed relation.[2] How could Russell decide *a priori* whether he might ever encounter a situation which had to be symbolized by a 27-termed relation? Of course, he could not; he could only decide such a thing after he had encountered all objects and seen what kinds of contexts they required. It may be that no relation can be less than 4-termed, or, quite the contrary, more than 4-termed.[3] If logic is kept properly non-empirical, an 'enumeration' of specific forms of elementary sentences can only be made arbitrarily.[4] Or, as Wittgenstein says, there is no privileged number.[5] The forms of sentences cannot be numbered;[6] it is impossible to claim that basically there is only *one* kind of elementary sentence, say, subject-predicate (it is this, I believe, which at 4.128b Wittgenstein calls 'philosophical monism'), or that basically there are only *two*, say, subject-predicate and dyadic relational ('philosophical dualism'). The use of such numbers in logic demands a justification, and since the justification is extra-logical, this is to say that there are no numbers in logic.[7]

All this is on the negative side: what logic cannot include. The positive side is that logic does include at least *general* information

---

[1] See Russell: *Our Knowledge of the External World*, esp. pp. 66–67, but also pp. 60–63; 'On Scientific Method in Philosophy', esp. p. 108; *The Philosophy of Logical Atomism*, esp. pp. 198–9. For possible indication that Russell accepted this criticism see *Principia Mathematica*, Introduction to Second Edition, p. xv.

[2] 5.5541.

[3] See G. E. Moore: op. cit., p. 296; cf. *LF* pp. 163–4, *Nbk.* 27.4.16.

[4] 5.554.        [5] 5.553b.        [6] 4.128a.

[7] 5.453; I have mentioned only Russell's hierarchy of dyadic, triadic, tetradic . . . relations, but Wittgenstein may also have had in mind the hierarchy from Russell's Theory of Types of first order, second order, third order . . . elementary sentences (see e.g. *LF* p. 163). It makes no difference; the argument applies in either case.

about elementary sentences,[1] and that it does not include the sorts of *specific* information I have just mentioned does not hamper logic. For logic is primarily interested in the system whereby we build symbols out of other, more basic symbols.[2] The basic symbols themselves, apart from a few general features, are a matter of indifference. The only hierarchy we can foresee in a logical theory is the one we ourselves construct,[3] that is to say, this hierarchy of symbols built from more basic ones in accordance with the rules of the system. A proper logical hierarchy, Wittgenstein says, is and must be independent of reality.[4]

Wittgenstein has another, perhaps clearer, way of making both positive and negative points. Logic, he says, deals not with the experience that something is so, but with the 'experience' that something is, that there do exist things (i.e. complexes and, as we can deduce, objects).[5] This is not an experience in the true sense, because an experience is always of particular complexes in some relation or other. Thus, logic precedes the How (how complexes and objects are arranged) but not the What (that there are complexes and so must be objects). Logic cannot precede this second sort of knowledge, because it is what gives form to its symbols. For example we know that '$x$', '$y$', &c., refer to objects, that '$p$', '$q$', &c., are combinations of these names, and that with the operation '$N(\xi)$' we can build from these names every possible assertion about the complexes which can be built from the objects.[6] If we did not know at least this much, Wittgenstein asks, how could we apply logic?[7] If the signs logic manipulates have no characteristics whatsoever, or only ones arbitrarily selected, then what makes us sure that the system applies to the world? Wittgenstein imagines someone's embarrassing us with the question: 'if there would be a logic even if there were no world, how then could there be a logic given that there is a world?' But in fact we are in no doubt that logic applies, because the symbols we have introduced into logic have been introduced either to describe complexes or to stand for objects.

---

[1] 5.555a.     [2] 5.555b.     [3] 5.556; cf. *Nbk.* 15.4.16a, 26.4.16a–c, 21.11.16a.
[4] 5.5561b; with 5.555–5.5561 compare *Nbk.* 15.4.16–27.4.16.
[5] 5.552a.     [6] See 4.24, 5.5a.     [7] 5.5521.

This is Wittgenstein's position on how much can be known about elementary sentences. It is not nearly as clear a position as its conciseness might suggest. The special 'experience' in logic is supposed to tell us that there are complexes. But does not knowing that there are complexes require experience in an ordinary sense? It would seem that only after some experience or other, i.e. *a posteriori*, could we possibly know this. Perhaps some of this Wittgenstein is willing to admit. In fact, it may be the point of his using the word 'experience' at all. But perhaps he thinks that there are reasons why this special 'experience' is not *a posteriori*, namely, that experiences in the *a posteriori* sense are of how things are in this world and that 'experience' is of what must be the case in any world. Perhaps the contrast here is between the contingent and the necessary. If so, the real unclarity of his position begins to appear. Why then cannot logic include knowledge of the forms of objects? Objects are eternal, so knowledge of their forms qualifies as knowledge of what will be the case in any world. In fact why, since their bearers are eternal, cannot logic include proper names? These may seem absurd questions, but all of Wittgenstein's arguments apply in their case as well. If *a* and *b* are objects, then the 'experience' that *a* and *b* exist is not an experience of how things stand; what we experience, in the ordinary sense of the word, are *a* and *b* in some relation or other. Obviously Wittgenstein does not intend this knowledge to be *a priori*, and I mention it to show that his criteria for what is *a priori* are not as clear as they could be. Again, I said that Wittgenstein seemed to think that it was possible to know *a priori* at least very general forms of objects and sentences, and he also seems to be extremely vague as to how general these forms must be. In the 6.3's he discusses the language of the natural sciences, and part of his argument, you will recall, is that many statements in science are not empirical, but are rather *a priori* intuitions of possible forms for empirical statements. The law of causality, for instance, is not an empirical law but a form which laws which are empirical may follow. So it is not only the much discussed general form of the sentence that we can know *a priori*; we can also know some of the more specific forms, some of the forms which sentences that describe the world may have. But does Wittgenstein ever tell us how specific we can get and still remain in the domain of forms knowable *a priori*?

I do not mean that Wittgenstein's position is not at all clear. The forms which, according to the 6.3's, we can intuit *a priori* are obviously fairly general ones; and the forms which, according to the 5.55's, we definitely cannot know *a priori* are the most specific ones: for example, whether there are dyadic, triadic, &c., relations. So, it is clear that Wittgenstein's position is something like this. Never in the *Tractatus* does he give or intentionally suggest an example of an elementary sentence or of an object, and the *Tractatus* is neutral on all questions which would require knowledge of an example for their solution; furthermore, he does at places give certain very general forms of objects and of elementary sentences. However, it seems to me quite unclear where the line between specific and general is to be drawn. Agnosticism about elementary sentences is, for this reason, not an entirely comfortable position. In this situation the wisest procedure (as it probably is in any case) is to take each part of the *Tractatus* on its own merits and to get as much information out of it as, within reason, one can.

It is surprising how much this procedure turns up, even from a place like the 5.55's. For example, 5.5563 goes:

In fact, all the sentences of our everyday language, just as they stand, are in perfect logical order.—That utterly simple thing, which we have to formulate here, is not an image of the truth, but the truth itself in its entirety.

(Our problems are not abstract, but perhaps the most concrete that there are.)

This is one of the passages Wittgenstein discusses in *Philosophical Investigations*, where he provides this helpful gloss:[1]

Thought is surrounded by a halo.—Its essence, logic, presents an order, in fact the *a priori* order of the world: that is, the order of *possibilities*, which must be common to both world and thought. But this order, it seems, must be *utterly simple*. It is *prior* to all experience, must run through all experience; no empirical cloudiness or uncertainty can be allowed to affect it.—It must rather be of the purest crystal. But this crystal does not appear as an abstraction; but as something concrete, indeed, as the most concrete, as it were the *hardest* thing there is. (*Tractatus Logico-Philosophicus* 5.5563).

[1] *PI* para. 97.

What logic does is to present the parallel *a priori* orders of the world and of thought. In the case of thought, it is the order of significant sentences, in the case of the world, of states of affairs; in either case it is, as Wittgenstein says, the order of possibilities. 5.5563 is a comment on what Wittgenstein says about hierarchies. The only hierarchies in logic are the ones it constructs: given '*p*' and '*q*' as elementary sentences (whatever their content may be), logic can construct a hierarchy by generating all possibilities from them. And the point of 5.5563 is that this sort of hierarchy is not abstract. It is the hardest thing there is, because it is the bones, the skeleton, of both the world and of thought.

Just before he makes this remark, Wittgenstein observes that all sentences in ordinary language are so far as logic goes, perfectly in order. There is the same juxtaposition of thoughts in the *Investigations*: from the passage just quoted he goes on to say:[1]

On the one hand it is clear that every sentence in our language 'is in order as it is'. That is to say, we are not *striving after* an ideal, as if our ordinary vague sentences had not yet got a quite unexceptionable sense, and a perfect language awaited construction by us.—On the other hand it seems clear that where there is sense there must be perfect order.— So there must be perfect order even in the vaguest sentence.

Ordinary sentences, then, are all right because they too are built up from elementary sentences. They have a hierarchical structure of their own; *therefore* they are all right. But why does this follow? Throughout these passages in the *Investigations* Wittgenstein seems to use 'vague sentence' as an equivalent for 'sentence in ordinary language'. Ordinary sentences are vague, because they leave things open.[2] And this is why Wittgenstein thinks there might be uneasiness about ordinary sentences in the first place: can a sentence with an incomplete sense really be a significant sentence? I have touched on this topic before in discussing 'indeterminateness of sense'.[3] Vagueness in sentences comes from generality. Consider a sentence like 'the watch is on the table' on a particular occasion of its use. Here, as with most ordinary sentences, we use descriptions, and descriptions may fit many things.

[1] *PI* para. 98; to understand 5.5562–5.5571 one should compare *PI* paras. 96–109 entire.
[2] *PI* para. 99.  [3] See Ch. vi.5–6.

We specify only that we mean objects structured so as to constitute, say, a watch, a table, &c.; but we leave unspecified the particular objects we mean. Wittgenstein's conclusion is that though ordinary sentences are indefinite (i.e. general) in sense, this does not make them logically suspect. We build them up out of elementary sentences; in the process we do drop out names and retain only forms, and thus in the process we do drop out part of the sense of the elementary sentences. But ordinary sentences are built up in accordance with the perfectly determinate order of logic; thus the part of the sense that does remain is perfectly definite.

This now explains 5.5562:

If we know on purely logical grounds that there must be elementary sentences, then everyone who understands sentences in their unanalysed form must know it.

Our ground for knowing that there must be elementary sentences is the necessity for definiteness of sense. There have to be names because otherwise we could not picture the world. But these are grounds which everyone must be aware of. This is not to say that everyone is aware of the existence of elementary sentences, but that everyone knows all that has to be known in order to prove it. When anyone hears a sentence like 'the watch is on the table', he knows that it does not specify all that it might. He also knows that it can be completely specific only by indicating each particular thing we mean. He knows also that this sentence has several other sentances logically subordinate to it; if it is true that 'the watch is on the table', then it is true that 'the wheel is on the table', 'the spring is on the table', &c., and that 'the legs are attached to the table top', &c. Indefiniteness of sense is plain to everyone, and this is all that logic uses to prove the existence of elementary sentences.

With 5.5562 explained, 5.557 is clear. Logic contains the skeletons of all sentences. But it is only when we bring this knowledge to bear on the world, when, in an analysis, we actually uncover the skeletons of the sentences, that we find what things fulfil the criteria of simple objects, and what elementary sentences there are.[1] So, logic cannot provide examples of elementary

[1] 5.557a.

sentences, because obviously what one can only discover by *applying* logic one cannot anticipate *in* logic.[1]

Thus, we can see from the 5.55's, first, that Wittgenstein fails to produce examples, not because analysis is something totally outside his acquaintance, but because actual analyses lie outside the bounds of logic. This leaves open the possibility that, though Wittgenstein may never have concerned himself much with actual analyses, he may still have had a fairly good idea of their possible results. The 5.55's also show that Wittgenstein knows that there are elementary sentences not because he has examples of them but because he has a proof.[2] Determinateness of sense requires them. And this proof shows something too. Analysis is reduction from reference to complex *objects* to reference to simple *objects*, but the reference is always to objects. Analysis is movement from speaking about that part of the world we can only describe, to that part of the world we can simply name, but in either case we are speaking of the world.

These last few remarks bring to light the two most important features of Wittgenstein's logical atomism. First, the *only* ground Wittgenstein gives for his concern with analysis is that a sentence's sense is complete only when expressed in terms of elementary sentences. His preoccupation, that is, is with completeness and incompleteness in the description of the world; it is *not* with impressions and ideas. This leads on to the second feature. Wittgenstein's sentences, whether elementary or not, are descriptions of the world. They are not reports of sense-data, and the long philosophical tradition whose concern is with sense-data is not his tradition. These two features can be summed up: analysis is reduction to what is basic, not in experience, but in reference.

## 3. *Elementary Sentences and Sense-Data*

I tentatively reached this conclusion, you may recall, when discussing the picture theory. I argued then that at least some of the pictures and models Wittgenstein had in mind must have been of the kind Hertz uses in *The Principles of Mechanics*. Hertz's models,

---

[1] 5.557b; see also 5.5571.     [2] Cf. *Nbk*. 23.5.15i.

of course, have nothing to do with sense-data; their function is to report on the world, in the sense we ordinarily think of the natural sciences as doing. Then, since Wittgenstein identifies the totality of true statements with the complete natural science, *all* statements, it very much seems, are this type of report about the world. The only thing that held me back earlier was the thought that, though this might be Wittgenstein's own way of reading the *Tractatus*, he may have intended his account to be general enough to permit of other, e.g. sense-datum, readings as well. But that the *Tractatus* has nothing to do with sense-data, I want now to maintain, is almost certain. Two short arguments, I believe, settle the matter. First, Wittgenstein is perfectly explicit that objects, as he means the term, are what constitute facts,[1] and that facts, as he means the term, are what constitute the world.[2] And there is no possibility that 'the world' can be read as 'the world of my experience'; he means, he says, reality.[3] Second, objects are eternal,[4] and this would hardly be the case with the parts of a sense-datum.

In short, the 'this red now' variety of sentence is not elementary, and it fails not from any minor defect but because it comes from entirely the wrong philosophical tradition. Wittgenstein's tradition is, in a way, not even a philosophical one; his aim is to state the logical features of reports about the world, and he seems to regard the models which Hertz, Watson, Toulmin, and others discuss not as one among many kinds of picture of the world, but as the archetype of pictures generally. This brings me back to what I said in the first chapter about Hertz. Hertz saw only the outlines of a picture theory, and it took the talent we normally associate with Wittgenstein to turn it into what we find in the *Tractatus*. This is why I said then that Wittgenstein's debt to Hertz was not on a par with his debt to Frege—or to Russell, for that matter. But I also said that Frege's influence was on the content of the *Tractatus* and that Hertz was the important influence on its form. We associate less a settled doctrine with Frege than an interest in certain questions, and what doctrine he had was not of the breadth to be compared with the system Wittgenstein built. Russell did have doctrines of this breadth, but it has been one of

[1] 2.01, 2.0272.    [2] 1.1, 1.11, 2.04.    [3] 2.063.    [4] 2.027, 2.0271.

my main contentions that it is a great mistake to assimilate Witt-genstein's atomistic system with Russell's. Of the three, Hertz seems to provide the best comparison. Hertz, like Wittgenstein, was interested in systematically setting out the principles to which reports about the world, in the straightforward sense of this phrase, must conform. He also seems to have thought, as did Wittgenstein, that ultimately all assertions reduce to assertions about simple, 'indestructible' objects. On this last point, however, Wittgenstein's reasons were quite different from Hertz's; Wittgen-stein's reasons, which I now want to look at more closely and more critically, were purely logical: we must be able to reduce to objects, he thought, for otherwise there would be no determinate-ness of sense.

## 4. *Wittgenstein's Logical Atomism*

The point Wittgenstein makes with his distinction between 'Satz' and 'sinnvoller Satz' is that the same sentence can be used on different occasions to make different claims about the world.[1] It is only with the *use* of a sentence that its expressions come to refer to things in the world, and it is only with successful reference that sentences come to have sense. I have said that Wittgenstein's proof that there are simples rests on the claim that there must be determinateness of sense.[2] Suppose I say to someone 'the watch is on the table'. Now I mean something perfectly definite, and something different from what another person using the same sentence but referring to a different watch and table would mean; and *I* know what I mean and normally *my hearer* knows what I mean. This is what Wittgenstein calls the 'sense' of the sentence.[3] Yet my sentence uses only descriptions. It is a proto-picture, in that it can be used to make claims different from mine. Thus we have, on the one hand, my particular sense, my picture of the world and, on the other, a mere proto-picture, something indefinite as to sense. It is here that Wittgenstein's argument begins. So long as there are descriptions in my sentence, I have only a proto-picture, i.e. something which can express many senses. It is only when I do away with descriptions *altogether*, therefore, that I shall

---

[1] See Ch. x.1.       [2] See Ch. vi.6.       [3] See Chs. vi.5, x.1.

have a picture, i.e. something which expresses my particular sense. This shows the force of the word 'picture' in at least certain contexts in the *Tractatus*; in these contexts Wittgenstein means by 'picture' something as detailed as a mirror image. This is how to read his claim that without substance it would be impossible to form a picture of the world.[1] Without things in the world which can be named, there can be no pictures in this strong sense. Yet, to complete the *modus tollens*, it is obvious that I do express my sense; my hearer usually understands me. It is a fact about the world that pictures in the strong sense pass back and forth between people. Therefore, there are simples, and names refer to the simples, and through the reference of these names we can depict particular facts. The point I made earlier may be clearer if I repeat it now: Wittgenstein is struggling in the *Tractatus* with problems of reference, not problems of knowledge.

Some of the questionable steps in this proof probably begin now to show themselves, but before I go into them, I want to have one last, brief look at objects. I have been suggesting that things like material points are objects.[2] I take it these are the spatial objects Wittgenstein talks about.[3] That is, were someone to press me for the picture behind my assertion 'the watch is on the table' (though, of course, no one ever does), in the analysis of the spatial dimensions of the assertion I should finally have to talk about material points. For example, in the analysis of my reference to the table I should have to talk about all the material points which compose it. This would seem to make analysis extraordinarily long, but evidently this is what Wittgenstein's analysis is like. It was like this in the *Notebooks* at any rate:[4]

A proposition like 'this chair is brown' seems to say something enormously complicated, for if we wanted to express this proposition in such a way *that nobody could raise objections to it on grounds of ambiguity*, it would have to be infinitely long.

Then, I have a number of times suggested that there are temporal objects.[5] Wittgenstein refers to them too often for the idea to be

---

[1] 2.0212.     [2] See Ch. VI.4; see also Chs. VII.3, XI.2.
[3] See 2.0121d, 2.0131a, 2.0251.     [4] *Nbk.* 19.9.14; my italics.
[5] See Ch. VI.4; see also Ch. VII.3.

ignored.[1] Indeed it seems to me that Wittgenstein would have to have them. The verb in 'the watch is on the table' is tensed, and the grounds for having to analyse the spatial dimension of my assertion would equally seem to be grounds for having to analyse its temporal dimension. I should have ultimately to say that I was making the claim about the watch's being on the table for *these* particular moments. In fact, it would seem that there would be, for Wittgenstein, many kinds of objects—namely, the simple parts of all the kinds of things to which we refer in our sentences. Should we refer to sounds, for example, the analysis of our statements would have to reduce to talk about the simple parts of the sounds.[2] I do not say that the *Tractatus* goes so far as to claim that there *are* different kinds of objects because this would be an empirical claim. But I think it does, by implication, say that for as many different kinds of complexes as there are, there will be equally many kinds of objects.

Another question I raised sometime earlier[3] was whether objects were simple in a logical or an ontological sense—whether they are defined by the finest mesh we, as language users, impose on the world, or whether they are already there in the world independently of us. The difficulty here is not lack of evidence, but the evidence's being so evenly divided. For example, what makes the logical view attractive is that it is all the proof of simplicity, on the face of it, justifies; and also that, if objects were ontologically simple, it seems doubtful whether they would any longer play the role the *Tractatus* has assigned then. For how is one going to *name* a sub-microscopic entity which could not possibly be an object of acquaintance? But, then, what makes the ontological view attractive are Wittgenstein's remarks about objects' forming the substance of the world, being unalterable, remaining the same through all change. How could some macroscopic object of acquaintance be that? In fact, so equally attractive, or unattractive, do each of these views look one is tempted, I think, to try combining them. The proof of simplicity, one might say, granting a point to the logical view, does only show there to be

---

[1] See *Nbk.* 22.5.15c, 2.0121d, 2.0251, *LF* p. 165.
[2] See *Nbk.* 11.9.16c, 2.0131b.          [3] See Ch. VII.3.

simples in the sense of things we can *refer to* without indeterminateness of sense, but perhaps, granting now a point to the ontological view, it is only *materially simple* things that permit of such reference. In this event, Wittgenstein would rightly consider a proof of the necessity of the former a proof of the necessity of the latter. Now, of the three alternatives I prefer the last. I think it has these two considerable recommendations. First, it is some recommendation that it brings a greater measure of coherence to the *Tractatus* than either of the other alternatives. Then, second, there is independent evidence, evidence on the crucial matter as to whether Wittgenstein thought only material simples yielded determinateness of sense, in the attack on logical atomism at the start of the *Investigations*. The atomism Wittgenstein attacks there holds the following. (i) *Real* names have meaning *only* by referring to objects.[1] (It is exactly this, I think, that the *Tractatus* proof of simplicity is supposed to show.) The sword Excalibur, to take Wittgenstein's example,[2] is the sort of thing that can be *both* named *and* described; we know what the name 'Excalibur' refers to only through some description, only by being told it is the name of the (whole) sword. So it functions somewhat analogously to the expression 'that sword', and sentences containing it will be indeterminate in sense. Hence, there must be things of a sort which can *only* be named, because only in that way will sense be determinate. Now, what is interesting is that Wittgenstein passes from this characteristic of the primary elements to two further characteristics. (ii) The elements cannot be said either to exist or not to exist, for existing or not existing consists in the holding or not holding of connexions between elements.[3] (iii) Elements are timeless, indestructible; because everything we call destruction lies in the separation of elements.[4] But notice that the elements, as Wittgenstein speaks of them in (ii) and (iii), are ontologically simple. The properties he attributes to them there hold, it would seem, only for material simples. How, then, has he managed this move from elements which can only be named to materially simple elements? He never tells us, but perhaps he would justify it like

---

[1] *PI* paras. 46, 49.  
[3] *PI* paras. 50, 58; cf. 79.  
[2] *PI* paras. 39, 44.  
[4] *PI* paras. 50, 58, 59.

this. Suppose *C* were materially complex. Then *C* could be described, because we could say that it is certain simpler items in a certain configuration. Thus, *C* could be both described and named. And since real names refer to objects which can only be named, they have to refer to material simples. But being materially simple is not quite the same as being indestructible. This feature is added because, on this view, it must be possible to describe the state of affairs in which everything destructible is destroyed, and this would only be possible if the things which are the meanings of the real names were themselves immune from destruction.[1]

So, the atomism described in the *Investigations* does involve passing from logical matters to a factual conclusion. And I believe that in this respect the atomism Wittgenstein describes is his own. Of course, arguing to the atomism of the *Investigations* has its pitfalls, if only because what Wittgenstein was doing there was not so much presenting any one person's position as sketching a whole philosophical tradition, from Plato and Augustine to Russell and himself. But my calculations in this case are roughly these. It is quite plain that the material simplicity and indestructibility of these elements are not modelled on Russell's 'individuals'.[2] And considering how much time Wittgenstein devotes to this side of the elements I doubt that he is interested simply in something out of the history of philosophy. Finally, when one recalls how much the *Investigations* remarks on indestructibility echo *Tractatus* claims about objects' never altering, surviving all change, and so forth, one is inclined, I think, to accept that they do represent Wittgenstein's own views. I have said that one would bring a greater measure of coherence to *Tractatus* doctrines, if one read it this way. Though the accommodation, I must now admit, is not complete. It is still not clear how one would name material simples. On my interpretation naming would have to be totally divorced from acquaintance, and Wittgenstein's names would be even further from ordinary ones than Russell's logically proper names. But lest this make one consider retreating and withdrawing

[1] *PI* para. 55.
[2] See Russell: *The Philosophy of Logical Atomism*, esp. pp. 200–3.

ontological status from objects, one should remember that this just means a return to a logical interpretation of simplicity with its own, perhaps even greater difficulties. The least unsatisfactory move I can find is to invoke a familiar formula. Perhaps how naming is actually accomplished is another of those *a posteriori* matters logicians need not concern themselves with; elementary particles must be, so evidently they can be, named.

This invocation, supposing it is Wittgenstein's, may not settle many doubts. But I believe that considerably more important defects in his proof of simplicity have begun to emerge; so I want to return to the proof.

Now, the proof itself contains much that is undeniable. When I say 'the watch is on the table', I mean a particular watch on a certain table at a point in time, and Wittgenstein is right to say that I can and do communicate this fully definite sense. I give my hearer a *picture* of the world. He is also quite right to think that how I manage to communicate such particular information with my general sentence very much needs accounting for. But does the fact that I *communicate* so much about the world with my sentence mean that my sentence *says* this much about the world—in the sense of *say* which Wittgenstein claims, namely, that my sentence can be analysed into sentences which, in aggregate, state all that was communicated by the original sentence? This seems to be Wittgenstein's fundamental, unexamined, and indefensible assumption. What language expresses (in the sense of communicates) language must be able to express (in the sense of make unambiguous through words). Or, to put this another way, since we communicate fully definite senses, ambiguity of reference is banishable. This is clearly so; my hearer's understanding what I meant by 'the watch is on the table' in itself demonstrates that reference to particulars can succeed. But does the fact that ambiguity of reference is banishable mean that it is banishable in language, that there must be sentences (viz. elementary sentences) in which we speak of things so simple (viz. objects) that we can use words which as good as point to them (viz. names)? Stating it like this, the *non sequitur* is obvious, and if my interpretation is right, then it is the principal *non sequitur* of the *Tractatus*.

It was an easy step to take. For understandable reasons Wittgenstein decided to call the picture I communicate to my hearer the *sense* of my sentence. That he called it the sense, that it was the sense *of a sentence*, that it was what *language* communicated, led him, I think, to make the following two moves. He decided, and this perhaps legitimately, that if language could not name simples it would be unable to express this picture, and then he concluded, and this quite illegitimately, that therefore language must have such names. The idea that anything outside language might have a part in specifying sense appears not to have been examined. One might have remarked to Wittgenstein that usually when I say 'the watch is on the table' my hearer understands me because the context makes clear the table I mean and, let us suppose, my hearer then looks and sees the watch I mean. But Wittgenstein would say that I can, if I wish, express my sentence in such a way that all dependence on context is eliminated. In fact, he would go further. He would say that I can express the sentence in such a way that it is impossible for a hearer, except for lack of acquaintance with the objects I name, to interpret my sentence in any but the way I intend. Ambiguity will not only be banished; it will be impossible.

Putting his argument like this shows, I think, how in general terms one ought to respond to it. Mostly as a consequence of the claims that logical atomism has made, we have now begun to attend to the complexity of naming, to the role of context in making the reference of words clear, and to the difficulty of specifying unambiguous rules for the use of words. Whether naming can be entirely separate from describing has successfully been put in doubt, and we all know that once the priority of naming goes one of the foundations of logical atomism goes. But it is equally dubious, and this I think is still more to the point with the *Tractatus*, that one could explain the sense of any assertion completely. One would, of course, be able to elaborate on it. But then the names and descriptions which together one would use for the elaboration would themselves have to be explained. And could this ever be done fully in language? If one accepts that frequently there is an intimate connexion between explaining the meaning of a word and giving certain of the rules we follow in using it, then this question could be put as follows. Is it possible to specify these rules to the point where misinterpretation is impossible? Most likely not. Wittgenstein argues that without simples it would be impossible to *picture* the world. To this the proper response would seem to be: we do not, nor can we, nor—evidently—need we picture the world in this sense.

# BIBLIOGRAPHY

*1. Wittgenstein's Works*:

*Extracts from Letters to Russell*, Appendix III to *Notebooks 1914-1916* (see below).

*Notes on Logic, Jour. of Phil.*, vol. liv (1957); repr. as Appendix I to *Notebooks 1914-1916* (see below).

*Notes Dictated to G. E. Moore in Norway*, Appendix II to *Notebooks 1914-1916* (see below).

*Notebooks 1914-1916*, German text ed. by G. H. von Wright and G. E. M. Anscombe, with English trans. by G. E. M. Anscombe, Oxford, 1961.

*Tractatus Logico-Philosophicus, Annalen der Naturphilosophie*, 1921.
—— German text, with English trans. by C. K. Ogden, London, 1922; second impression with a few corrections, 1933.
—— German text, with English trans. by D. F. Pears and B. F. McGuinness, London, 1961.

'Some Remarks on Logical Form', *Proc. Arist. Soc.*, Suppl. vol. ix (1929).

Letter to the Editor, *Mind*, vol. xlii (1933).

*The Blue and the Brown Books*, Oxford, 1958.

*Philosophical Investigations*, German text ed. by G. E. M. Anscombe and R. Rhees, with English trans. by G. E. M. Anscombe, Oxford, 1953; second edition, Oxford, 1958.

*Remarks on the Foundations of Mathematics*, German text ed. by G. H. von Wright, R. Rhees, and G. E. M. Anscombe, with English trans. by G. E. M. Anscombe, Oxford, 1956.

*2. Interpretations of the* Tractatus, *or works which explain views Wittgenstein held in years immediately before or after writing the* Tractatus:

ALLAIRE, E. B.: '*Tractatus* 6.3751', *Analysis*, vol. 19 (1959).
—— 'Types and Formation Rules: A Note on *Tractatus* 3.334', *Analysis*, vol. 21 (1960).
—— 'Existence, Independence, and Universals', *Phil. Rev.*, vol. lxix (1960).

ANSCOMBE, G. E. M.: *An Introduction to Wittgenstein's Tractatus*, London, 1959..
—— 'Mr. Copi on Objects, Properties and Relations in the *Tractatus*', *Mind*, vol. lxviii (1959).

AYER, A. J.: 'Demonstration of the Impossibility of Metaphysics', *Mind*, vol. xlii (1934).

BARONE, F.: 'Il Solipsismo Linguistico di Ludwig Wittgenstein', *Filosofia*, vol. 2 (1951).

—— 'Ludwig Wittgenstein', *Enciclopedia Filosofica*, 1957.

BERNSTEIN, R. J.: 'Wittgenstein's Three Languages', *Rev. of Metaphysics*, vol. xv (1961).

BERGMANN, G.: *The Metaphysics of Logical Positivism*, New York, 1954.

—— 'Intentionality', Semantica, Archivio di Filosofia, (1955).

—— 'The Revolt Against Logical Atomism', I and II, *Phil. Quar.*, vols. 7 (1957) and 8 (1958).

BLACK, M.: *The Nature of Mathematics*, London, 1933.

—— 'Some Problems Connected with Language', *Proc. Arist. Soc.*, vol. xxxix (1938); repr. as 'Wittgenstein's *Tractatus*' in *Language and Philosophy*, Ithaca, 1949.

—— Introduction to *Philosophical Analysis*, ed. by M. Black, Ithaca, 1950.

BLANSHARD, B.: *Reason and Analysis*, London, 1962.

BUTCHVAROV, P.: 'On an Alleged Mistake of Logical Atomism', *Analysis*, vol. 19 (1959).

CARNAP, R.: *The Logical Syntax of Language*, trans. by A. Smeaton, London, 1937.

CHADWICK, J. A.: 'Logical Constants', *Mind*, vol. xxxvi (1927).

COLOMBO, G. C. M.: critical introduction and notes to his translation of the *Tractatus*, Milano-Roma, 1954.

COPI, I. M.: 'Objects, Properties, and Relations in the *Tractatus*', *Mind*, vol. lxvii (1958).

—— 'Tractatus 5.542', *Analysis*, vol. 18 (1958).

DAITZ, E.: 'The Picture Theory of Meaning', repr. in *Essays in Conceptual Analysis*, ed. by Antony Flew, London, 1956.

DALY, C. B.: 'New Light on Wittgenstein', *Phil. Studies*, St. Patrick's College, Maynooth, Ireland, 1960.

EVANS, E.: 'Tractatus 3.1432', *Mind*, vol. lxiv (1955).

—— 'About "*aRb*" ', *Mind*, vol. lxviii (1959).

FEIBLEMAN, J. K.: *Inside the Great Mirror: A Critical Examination of the Philosophy of Russell, Wittgenstein, and Their Followers*, The Hague, 1958.

GARDINER, P.: *Schopenhauer*, Penguin Books, 1963.

D. A. T. G(ASKING) and A. C. J(ACKSON): 'Ludwig Wittgenstein', memorial notice, *Austr. Jour. of Phil.*, vol. xxix (1951).

GASKING, D. A. T.: 'Professor Anderson and the *Tractatus Logico-Philosophicus*', *Austr. Jour. of Phil.*, vol. xxvii (1949).

GEACH, P. T.: review of Italian edition and translation of the *Tractatus* by G. C. M. Colombo, *Phil. Rev.*, vol. lxvi (1957).

HAMBURG, C. H.: 'Whereof One Cannot Speak', *Jour. of Phil.*, vol. 1 (1953).

HARTNACK, J.: *Wittgenstein og den moderne filosofi*, Copenhagen, 1960; also trans. *Wittgenstein und die moderne Philosophie*, Stuttgart, 1962.

HAWKINS, D. J. B.: 'Wittgenstein and the Cult of Language', Aquinas Paper No. 27, Blackfriars Publications, 1957.

HINTIKKA, J.: 'On Wittgenstein's Solipsism', *Mind*, vol. lxvii (1958).

—— 'Identity, Variables, and Impredicative Definitions', *Jour. of Sym. Logic*, vol. xxi (1956).

KEYT, D.: 'Wittgenstein's Notion of an Object', *Phil. Quar.*, vol. 13 (1963).

KNEALE, W. and KNEALE, M.: *The Development of Logic*, Oxford, 1962.

KRAFT, V.: *The Vienna Circle*, trans. by A. Pap, New York, 1953.

LANGFORD, C. H.: 'On Propositions Belonging to Logic', *Mind*, vol. xxxvi (1927).

LANGER, S. K.: *Philosophy in a New Key*, New York, 1948.

LAZEROWITZ, M.: 'Tautologies and the Matrix Method', *Mind*, vol. xlvi (1937).

MALCOLM, N.: *Ludwig Wittgenstein: A Memoir*, London, 1958.

MASLOW, A.: *A Study in Wittgenstein's Tractatus*, Berkeley and Los Angeles, 1963.

MAYS, W.: 'Note on Wittgenstein's Manchester Period', *Mind*, vol. lxiv (1955).

—— 'Wittgenstein's Manchester Period', *The Guardian*, 24 March 1961.

McGUINNESS, B. F.: 'Pictures and Form in Wittgenstein's *Tractatus*', Archivio di Filosofia, (1956).

McTAGGART, J. E.: 'Propositions Applicable to Themselves', *Mind*, vol. xxxii (1923).

MOORE, G. E.: 'Wittgenstein's Lectures in 1930–33', repr. in *Philosophical Papers*, London, 1959.

MOORE, W.: 'Structure in Sentence and in Fact', *Phil. of Science*, vol. v (1938).

MURE, G. R. C.: *Retreat from Truth*, Oxford, 1958.

OGDEN, C. K. and RICHARDS, I. A.: *The Meaning of Meaning*, London, 1923.

PALMER, H.: 'The Other Logical Constant', *Mind*, vol. lxvii (1958).

PASSMORE, J.: *A Hundred Years of Philosophy*, London, 1957.
PEARS, D. F.: 'Logical Atomism: Russell and Wittgenstein',
    in *The Revolution in Philosophy*, intro. by G. Ryle, London,
    1956.
PLOCHMANN, G. K. and LAWSON, J. B.: *Terms in their Propositional
    Contexts   in   Wittgenstein's   'Tractatus':   An   Index*,
    Carbondale, 1962.
POPPER, K.: 'Ein Kriterium des empirischen Charakters theo-
    retischer Systeme', *Erkenntnis*, vol. iii (1933).
—— *The Open Society and Its Enemies*, London, 1945.
—— 'Philosophy of Science', in *British Philosophy in the Mid-
    Century*, ed. by C. A. Mace, London, 1957.
PROCTOR, G. L.: 'Scientific Laws, Scientific Objects and the
    *Tractatus*', *Brit. Jour. for Phil. of Science*, vol. x (1959).
RAMSEY, F. P.: critical notice of the *Tractatus*, repr. in *The
    Foundations of Mathematics, and Other Essays*, ed. by R. B.
    Braithwaite, London, 1931.
—— 'The Foundations of Mathematics', repr. as above.
—— 'Mathematical Logic', repr. as above.
—— 'Facts and Propositions', repr. as above.
RHEES, R.: 'Miss Anscombe on the *Tractatus*', *Phil. Quar.*, vol.
    10 (1960).
—— 'The *Tractatus*: Seeds of Some Misunderstandings', *Phil.
    Rev.*, vol. lxxii (1963).
RIVERSO, E.: *Ludwig Wittgenstein e il Simbolismo Logico*, Napoli,
    1956.
RUSSELL, B.: *The Philosophy of Logical Atomism*, repr. in *Logic and
    Knowledge*, ed. by R. C. Marsh, London, 1956.
—— Introduction to the *Tractatus*, London, 1922.
—— 'Logical Atomism', repr. in *Logic and Knowledge*, ed. by
    R. C. Marsh, London, 1956.
—— *An Inquiry into Meaning and Truth*, London, 1940.
—— 'Ludwig Wittgenstein', memorial notice, *Mind*, vol. lx (1951).
—— *My Philosophical Development*, London, 1959.
RYLE, G.: 'Ludwig Wittgenstein', memorial notice, *Analysis*,
    vol. 12 (1951).
SCHLICK, M.: 'The Turning Point in Philosophy', trans. by D.
    Rynin, repr. in *Logical Positivism*, ed. by A. J. Áyer,
    Glencoe, 1959.
—— 'Causality in Contemporary Physics', I and II, trans. by
    D. Rynin, *Brit. Jour. for Phil. of Science*, vol. xii (1961–2).
—— 'The Future of Philosophy', *Publ. in Phil. of the College of
    the Pacific*, 1932.

SCHWYZER, H. R. G.: 'Wittgenstein's Picture Theory of Language', *Inquiry*, vol. 5 (1962).

SELLARS, W.: 'Being and Being Known', *Proc. American Cath. Phil. Asso.*, 1960.

— 'Naming and Saying', *Phil. of Science*, vol. 29 (1962).

— 'Truth and "Correspondence" ', *Jour. of Phil.*, vol. lix (1962).

SHOEMAKER, S.: 'Logical Atomism and Language', *Analysis*, vol. 20 (1960).

SHWAYDER, D. S.: *Wittgenstein's 'Tractatus': A Historical and Critical Commentary*, a thesis for the degree of D.Phil. deposited in the Bodleian Library, Univ. of Oxford, 1954.

— Critical notice of Stenius: *Wittgenstein's 'Tractatus'*, *Mind*, vol. lxxii (1963).

STENIUS, E.: *Wittgenstein's 'Tractatus': A Critical Exposition of its Main Lines of Thought*, Oxford, 1960.

— 'Linguistic Structure and the Structure of Experience', *Theoria*, vol. xx (1954).

— 'Wittgenstein's Picture-Theory: A Reply to Mr. H. R. G. Schwyzer', *Inquiry*, vol. 6 (1963).

STERN, J. P.: *Lichtenberg, A Doctrine of Scattered Occasions*, Bloomington, 1959.

STIGEN, A.: 'Interpretations of Wittgenstein', *Inquiry*, vol. 5 (1962).

TOULMIN, S.: *The Philosophy of Science*, London, 1953.

URMSON, J. O.: *Philosophical Analysis*, Oxford, 1956.

VAN PEURSEN, C. A.: 'Edmund Husserl and Ludwig Wittgenstein', *Jour. of Phil. and Phenom. Research*, vol. xx (1959).

WAISMANN, F.: 'Logische Analyse der Wahrscheinlichkeitsbegriffe', *Erkenntnis*, vol. i (1930–1).

— 'Über den Begriff der Identität', *Erkenntnis*, vol. vi (1936–7).

— 'Was ist Logische Analyse?', *Jour. of Unified Science (Erkenntnis)*, vol. vii (1939-40).

WARNOCK, G. J.: *English Philosophy Since 1900*, Oxford, 1958.

WATSON, W. H.: *On Understanding Physics*, Cambridge, 1938.

VON WRIGHT, G. H.: 'Ludwig Wittgenstein: A Biographical Sketch', repr. in Malcolm, N. (see above).

WEILER, G.: 'On Fritz Mauthner's Critique of Language', *Mind*, vol. lxvii (1958).

WEINBERG, J. R.: *An Examination of Logical Positivism*, London, 1936.

WISDOM, J.: 'Logical Constructions', *Mind*, vol. xl (1931)–vol. xlii (1933).

— 'Ludwig Wittgenstein, 1934–1937', *Mind*, vol. lxi (1952).

*3. Works other than the above which are cited in this book:*

BOSANQUET, B.: *Knowledge and Reality*, London, 1885.
—— *Logic*, Oxford, 1888.
—— *The Essentials of Logic*, London, 1895.
BRADLEY, F. H.: *The Principles of Logic*, second edition, London, 1928.
—— *Appearance and Reality*, London, 1893.
DUMMETT, M.: 'Nominalism', *Phil. Rev.*, vol. lxv (1956).
FREGE, G.: *Begriffschrift*, repr. in *Translations from the Philosophical Writings of Gottlob Frege*, ed. by P. Geach and M. Black, Oxford, 1952.
—— 'Function and Concept', repr. as above.
—— *Grundgesetze der Arithmetik*, repr. as above.
—— *The Foundations of Arithmetic*, trans. by J. L. Austin, Oxford, 1953.
HERTZ, H.: *Electric Waves*, trans. by D. E. Jones, London, 1893.
—— *The Principles of Mechanics*, trans. by D. E. Jones and J. T. Walley, New York, 1956.
MEINONG, A.: *Über Möglichkeit und Wahrscheinlichkeit*, Leipzig, 1915.
MOORE, G. E.: 'The Nature of Judgement', *Mind*, vol. viii (1899).
RUSSELL, B.: *The Principles of Mathematics*, London, 1937.
—— 'Mathematical Logic as Based on the Theory of Types', repr. in *Logic and Knowledge*, ed. by R. C. Marsh, London, 1956.
—— 'On Scientific Method in Philosophy', repr. in *Mysticism and Logic*, Penguin Books, 1953.
—— and Whitehead, A. N.: *Principia Mathematica*, second edition, Cambridge, 1925.
—— *Our Knowledge of the External World*, London, 1926.
RYLE, G.: 'Systematically Misleading Expressions', repr. in *Logic and Language*, First Series, ed. by Antony Flew, Oxford, 1952.
SEARLE, J.: 'Proper Names', *Mind*, vol. lxvii (1958).
STRAWSON, P. F.: 'On Referring', repr. in *Essays in Conceptual Analysis*, ed. by Antony Flew, London, 1956.

# INDEX